HOW TO BE BORN AGAIN

How to be Born Again

Billy Graham

Hodder & Stoughton
LONDON   SYDNEY   AUCKLAND

Copyright © Billy Graham, 1977
Foreword copyright © Maurice Rowlandson, 1997

First published in Great Britain in 1977

1 3 5 7 9 10 8 6 4 2

British Library Cataloguing in Publication Data
A record for this book is available from the British Library

ISBN 0 340 671 22 X

Offset by Avon Dataset Ltd, Bidford-on-Avon, Warks
Printed and bound in Great Britain by
Cox & Wyman, Reading, Berks

Hodder and Stoughton
A division of Hodder Headline PLC
338 Euston Road
London NW1 3BH

Contents

PREFACE   vii

FOREWORD BY MAURICE ROWLANDSON   xiii

I. MAN'S PROBLEM   1

1. Why Am I So Empty?   3
2. Can Anyone Tell Me Where to Find God?   14
3. Does God Really Speak to Us?   21
4. But I'm Not Religious!   35
5. What Is This Thing Called Sin?   50
6. Does God Have a Cure for Spiritual Disease?   62

II. GOD'S ANSWER   77

7. The Man Who Is God   79
8. What Happened at the Cross   91
9. The King's Courtroom   100
10. Jesus Christ Is Alive   114

III. MAN'S RESPONSE   125

11. The New Birth Is for Now   127
12. The New Birth Is Not Just a "Feeling"   138
13. Alive and Growing   154

NOTES   171

Preface

TODAY BEING "born again" is big news. *Time* magazine carries a feature story on "Born Again Faith."[1] Political candidates give the subject as much attention as the latest economic statistics or the energy crisis. A former Black Panther leader and radical of the 1960s returns from exile and announces, "My life has turned 180 degrees. I have been born again." A man who was deeply involved in one of the most publicised political scandals of our time writes a best seller explaining the change in his life as a result of being born again. A Gallup poll comes up with the astonishing conclusion that in the United States "more than one-third of those who are old enough to vote have experienced 'born again' religious conversions."[2]

Born again!

Is it possible? Can life be transformed?

What's it all about? What does it mean?

Is it real? Will it last?

How is a person "born again"?

The expression "born again" is not a new term, invented by modern journalists to describe recent religious trends. The term "born again" is almost two thousand years old. One dark night, in the ancient city of Jerusalem, Jesus turned to one of the best-known intellectuals of his time and said, "I say to you, unless one is born again, he cannot see the kingdom of God" (John 3:3). In those words Jesus told us of both the necessity and the possibility of new birth—of spiritual transformation. Since that time untold millions throughout the ages have attested to the reality and the power of God in their lives through being born again.

A young Marine Corps officer, a veteran of the Vietnam War, described publicly the night battle in Vietnam when he and his troops came under enemy attack. Only a few were lifted out alive by helicopter. The sixteen surgical operations he endured had helped to restore his physical powers, but now he was speaking of the spiritual rebirth he had received since returning home. He said, "We bear an allegiance to the flag of our country, but unless we have been born again through faith in Christ, all our religion is worth nothing."

This lieutenant had been born again.

I think of the great Dutch Christian, Corrie ten Boom, who is now in her 80s. Her story of courage in the midst of the Nazi persecution has inspired millions. She tells of an experience when she was only five years old when she said, "I want Jesus in my heart." She described how her mother took her little hand in hers and prayed with her. "It was so simple, and yet Jesus Christ says that we all must come as children, no matter what our age, social standing, or intellectual background."[3]

Corrie ten Boom, at the age of five, had been born again.

I have had countless people tell me, in person and by letter, how they were born again and their lives were changed. A man from Milwaukee wrote, "Tonight my wife and I had come to the brink of ending our marriage. We felt we could no longer stay together under the conditions in which we were living. Both of us admitted that we thought we no longer loved each other. I no longer enjoyed her company nor appreciated my home life. We made bitter statements about each other. We could make no compromise, nor could we agree on how to improve our marriage even if we were to try.

"I believe it was God's will that I turned on the television and listened to your message about spiritual rebirth. As my wife watched with me, we began to search our hearts and felt a new life within us. I prayed that God would come into my heart and truly make me a new man and help me begin a new life. Our troubles seem rather slight now."

Both this man and his wife were born again.

What does it mean to be born again? It is not just a remodelling job, performed somehow by us on ourselves. Today we hear a lot about recycling, reconstruction, and reshaping. We renovate houses and add on more rooms. We tear down old buildings and build new ones in our cities, calling it urban renewal. Millions and millions of dollars are spent every year on health spas, beauty resorts, and exotic cosmetics—all by people hoping to reshape their faces or renew their bodies.

In like manner, people frantically pursue all sorts of promised cures for the renewal of their inner lives. Some people hunt for renewal at the psychiatrist's office. Others search for spiritual renewal in exotic oriental religions or processes of inward meditation. Still others seek for inner peace and renewal in drugs or alcohol. Whatever the path, however, they eventually come to a dead end. Why? Simply because man cannot renew himself. God created us. Only God can recreate us. Only God can give us the new birth we so desperately want and need.

I believe this is one of the most important subjects in the entire world. Governments may be elected or may topple. Military machines may advance and retreat. Men may explore outer space or probe the ocean depths. All of these events are part of the grand plan for humans on this planet.

But the central theme of the universe is the purpose and destiny of every individual. Every person is important in God's eyes.

That is why God is not content to stand with His arms folded (as it were) and simply watch the human race wallow in misery and destruction. The greatest news in the universe is that we can be born again! "For God so loved the world, that He gave His only begotten Son, that whoever believes in Him should not perish, but have eternal life" (John 3:16).

This new birth happens in all kinds of ways. It may seem to happen over a period of time or in a moment. The paths which people take to reach that point of decision may be very direct or very circuitous. Whatever the path, we always find Christ at the end to welcome us. And that encounter with Christ, that new birth, is the beginning of a whole new path in life under His control. Lives can be remarkably changed, marriages excitingly improved, societies influenced for good—all by the simple, sweeping surge of individuals knowing what it is to be born again.

It may be that down inside you sense an unnamed need you cannot describe. Perhaps you have been consciously searching all your life to fill a void in your heart and to find a purpose for living. Perhaps outwardly you have been very successful in life, but you know it has not brought you peace and true happiness. Perhaps your life is an unbroken chain of heartaches and shattered dreams. Maybe you are just curious.

Whatever your background may be, I pray that God will use this little book to give you hope—to show you that you, too, can be born again.

How to Be Born Again is not for the theologians or the philosophers. There are many learned works of theology which probe the meaning of the new birth (or "regeneration," as theologians often call it). I know there have been different emphases among theologians concerning the new birth. Some have stressed the importance of what God does to bring us to faith. Some have stressed the importance of man's search for faith. Some have thought of the new birth as a single event in time, while others use the term to speak of all God wills to do in our lives. Ultimately there is a mystery about the new birth; we cannot understand everything about it, for our minds are finite.

However much the theologians may disagree about fine points of doctrine, the central truth of the new birth is clear: Man apart from God is spiritually dead. He needs to be born again. Only by God's grace through faith in Christ can this new birth take place.

My concern has been to make this book practical. Although we may not be able to say everything possible about the new birth, I have wanted to say everything that was necessary to help people who really want to know God. I want to help them come to have this life-changing experience. I want them—I want you—to be born again. I believe God wants you to be born again.

We were already working on this book when the term "born again" became big news. I have sensed the blessing of God as we have continued writing, and have sensed also that God may have led us to write this book at just the right time as millions wonder about being born again.

I gave my original manuscript to my friend Carole Carlson— and asked for help. Then with the added help of my wife, of Millie Dienert, and of Cliff and Billie Barrows, we finished it in a little apartment in Mexico while I recuperated from an illness.

Thus, my deepest appreciation to Bill and Vivian Mead of Dallas, Texas, and our wonderful friends the Servitje family in Mexico for making our working, recuperating period possible; to my secretary Stephanie Wills, who typed and retyped the manuscript; for the wonderful encouragement and help from my wife, Ruth; for the comments of my colleague Dr. John Akers; but especially to Carole Carlson for the magnificent work she did in helping me to simplify what could have been too deep and theological for people all over the world who I pray will read this book and experience "the new birth."

BILLY GRAHAM

Montreat, North Carolina
May 1, 1977

Foreword

Timeless words for a timeless experience: BORN AGAIN. It was the American President Jimmy Carter who recently popularised the words again and brought them into prominence in our generation. In so doing, he was but a latter-day Nicodemus.

'You must be born again,' said the Lord Jesus Christ to that first-century ruler. Not that the words were easily understood. 'How can I go through the experience of birth again?' he asked. To his trained and logical mind the theological simplicity of a new birth was more than he could assimilate. Until, that is, the Lord Jesus Christ made the profound yet startlingly simple statement that 'God so loved the world, that He gave His only begotten Son, that whosoever believeth in Him should not perish, but have everlasting life' (John 3:16 KJV).

That those words established an understanding in the mind of Nicodemus is clear from the later mention of him in the Gospels. He was undoubtedly one who, through Christ's own ministry, was 'born again'.

And those words have echoed and re-echoed through the centuries to reach us today. Our terminology may be different; we talk about 'committing your life to Christ' or 'giving your heart to Jesus'. But it has the same connotation – we need to be 'born again'.

St Augustus, in early Anglo-Saxon times, talked about being born again. Wesley and Whitefield went across the whole of England and America preaching the importance of a new birth in Christ Jesus. Moody and Sankey, at the turn of the present century, had nothing but the same message, and they were followed, in the 1930s, by the powerful rough diamond Gypsy Smith. The 1939–45 war was a time when evangelism largely lay dormant (but for the United States Army Gospel Song Team).

In 1945 a young evangelist by the name of Tom Rees, on his own initiative, took over Central Hall, Westminster, for the entire month of September and told the gospel-starved young people of the capital, 'You need to be born again.' Later he filled London's Royal Albert Hall more than fifty times to thunder out the same message.

Meanwhile, from America news was reaching Britain of another outstanding young evangelist who had conducted a 'Crusade' in a tent in Los Angeles. Many thousands, it was reported, had responded to his message: that they must be 'born again'. Indeed, it was said that the Crusade had been extended because of the crowds that continued to come. Famous people like Olympic medallist Louis Zamperini, wiretapper Jim Vaus and newscaster Stuart Hamblen responded to the invitation to be born again. The newspaper magnate Randolph Hearst issued his now famous edict to his journalists to 'puff Graham' (that simply meant that they were to feature him – and commend him – in their columns).

As a result, in 1952 about 170 British Christian leaders were called together in Church House, Westminster, to hear Billy Graham tell of his ministry and of the way in which God had been blessing the proclamation of the old-fashioned gospel message.

His address was published in a booklet entitled *The Work of an Evangelist* and a copy was sent to every minister and clergyman in the UK. From that meeting grew the 1954 Greater London Crusade, which ran for twelve weeks at London's Harringay Arena. Billy Graham – himself a former Youth for Christ evangelist – had a different message for each night, but the underlying message was always the same: 'You must be born again.' In a further twenty-two Crusades and Missions throughout the British Isles his message has never varied. 'The Bible says . . .' he has proclaimed, with pointing finger and Bible held high, '. . . you must be born again.'

'How?' is an appropriate question to ask. This book – first published in 1977 – is a clear and concise answer to that question. It is a book that can be given to anyone without apology, for it is direct and challenging. It is also appropriate that it should be republished at this time, as Billy Graham is approaching his eightieth birthday in 1998.

I have had the privilege of working for him and of travelling to many places across the world in association with his ministry. Everywhere I have gone there have been those who were quick to tell me of the significant effect his ministry has had upon their lives. They have all been 'born again' – not through Billy Graham, but through the power of the Holy Spirit as Graham has preached the Cross of Christ and challenged his listeners to commit their lives to Christ as their Saviour and Lord.

Now, through this book, his challenge is again communicated to the reader. There will be those who will look back on the reading of this book as the catalyst in their lives which brought them to find the 'salvation that is in Christ Jesus'. Their lives will be changed and they will be 'born again'.

MAURICE L. ROWLANDSON
July 1996

How to be Born Again

I

Man's Problem

1

Why Am I So Empty?

WHEN THE VIKING landed on Mars, the world exclaimed, "Unbelievable! Magnificent!" The mysterious Red Planet had been penetrated. An ingeniously designed robot which was the result of one billion dollars and the probing minds of hundreds of scientists had accomplished a task that man had dreamed about for generations.

Exploring the great mysteries of the universe, trying to predict the quirks of nature, attempting to predict a trend in society or politics are all modern concerns.

In the business world, for instance, men search for ways to improve their efficiency. On office walls and on bulletin boards of sales organisations we see slogans like "Plan Ahead" or "Plan Your Work and Work Your Plan." Corporations hire firms at large fees to determine how they can improve their planning. Business, world politics, and economics change so fast that in a few days the direction of an entire country can change. Companies called "Think Factories" project thinking a decade or more in advance to keep abreast of the changing times.

In our daily lives we keep a calendar, trying to mark down appointments and schedule our days. If there were no planning, children would never get to the dentist, mothers would never make the community meeting, businesses and labour unions would collapse. We are always searching for ways to streamline our lives, to simplify daily living.

But what about the greater issues of life and death? Do we plan? Do we need to search for answers to the deep moral and spiritual questions so that our lives are more orderly? Man has always thought so, which is why we have philosophers, psychologists, and theologians. Today, however, much of the world in search of knowledge and fulfillment ignores God!

I knew a brilliant young lawyer who did not seem to find a need for God during his intense years of concentration as a student. Later, he began to write a book about a famous person. While he was working on this book we had a conversation during the course of which I detected that he was on a personal spiritual quest. He hoped to find somewhere in the life of the man who was the subject of his book a spiritual fulfillment which he himself wanted. He knew this person believed in God and had accepted Christ into his heart. He also seemed reassured that the one about whom he was writing had doubts from time to time.

This young man who has been searching for so long has now become interested in spiritual things. In my earlier contacts with him I thought he was an agnostic, interested only in gaining knowledge at the university and later at law school. Now I suspect that all through adolescence and his twenties he was searching for God without knowing it.

THE SELF-MADE MAN

We are taught to be independent, to make it on our own. As we look at an individual we may say, "Now there's someone who's made it!" We admire him and respect his ability to "pull himself up by his bootstraps."

We have even had a well-known TV commercial that says, "Please, mother, I'd rather do it myself."

And yet within each of us is a deep-seated frustration: "I ought to be better. I believe I was made for something more; there must be more to life than this. Why am I so empty?"

Such feelings, often subconscious, cause us to struggle toward some unknown, unnamed goal. We may try to evade this quest, we may detour into a fantasy world, we may even regress to lower levels of life and seek to escape. We may throw up our hands in disgust and say, "What's the use? I'm O.K. just working and keeping out of trouble." But somehow, deep inside is a compulsion which invariably leads us to take up the search again.

This is one of the reasons the nation became fascinated by *Roots*, the product of Alex Haley's ten-year search for identity. Rod McKuen felt rootless and a strange "vacuum" in his heart as he began his search for his true father. The oldest book in the possession of the human race is Job, and Job once exclaimed, "Oh that I knew where I might find Him" (Job 23:3).

This search transcends race, age, economic status, sex, and educational background. Either man began nowhere and is looking for some place to go, or he began somewhere and lost his way. In either case, he's searching. None of us will ever find "total satisfaction" until we find that our roots are in eternity.

A famous scientist at an eastern university asked to see me. Somewhat surprised, I met him in a quiet room at the Student Union. Suddenly this brilliant man, admired by many and respected as a leader in his field, broke down. When he regained his composure he told me: "I'm at the point of ending my life.... My home is a wreck, I'm a secret alcoholic, my children don't respect me. I've never really had a guiding principle in my life except to be recognised in my field of physics. I've come to realise that I don't really know the true values of living. I've watched you on TV and although I don't understand all you're trying to communicate, I have a conviction that you know what the real meaning of life is."

He hesitated, and I'm sure the next thing this famous, self-made man said was very difficult for him: "I've come to you for help." It was a desperate cry.

From every culture, every country—from those who cannot read to Nobel Prize winners—there is the age-old phenomenon, the mystery of *anthropos*, the "upward-looking one," the one who is searching, inquiring for life's deeper and often hidden meaning.

In airports, on planes, in hotel lobbies across the world, people have come to me with serious questions about broken family relationships, ill health, or financial catastrophes. But more often they reveal empty souls. On an airplane flight a man poured out his life story to me. It was a saga of shattered dreams, broken hopes, and emptiness. Before we parted he had said "yes" to Christ. Tremendous relief came over his face as he whispered, "Thank you."

When we landed, I watched him embrace his wife and talk excitedly to her at the same time. I don't know what their conversation was, but from his expression he was evidently telling her of his new relationship with the Lord. I can only imagine how amazed she must have been at the change, because he had told me how his temper and unfaithfulness had just about broken their marriage.

I don't know if his marriage was put back together, because I never saw him again, but his direction was certainly changed on that plane trip.

FAME AND FORTUNE

One of our best-known show biz personalities asked me to come to his dressing room after a show on which I had appeared. He motioned me in and said, "I make people laugh ... but inside I feel like hell. I've been married twice; both marriages have broken up. It's been mostly my fault, I guess, but I don't think I could make a go of a third marriage unless I could find some sort of fulfillment which I don't know how to get."

He stopped and looked at me. "Do you think what I'm really looking for is summed up in the word *God*?"

All of his fame and money had not satisfied his searching heart.

A man who was destined to be very influential in the life of Charles Colson, of Watergate fame; was Tom Phillips. Colson writes in his book, *Born Again*, that Phillips said: " 'It may be hard to understand.... But I didn't seem to have anything that mattered. It was all on the surface. All the material things in life are meaningless if a man hasn't discovered what's underneath them....

" 'One night I was in New York on business and noticed that Billy Graham was having a Crusade in Madison Square Garden.' Tom continued. 'I went—curious, I guess—hoping maybe I'd find some answers. What Graham said that night put it all into place for me. I saw what was missing—the personal relationship with Jesus Christ, the fact that I hadn't ever asked Him into my life, hadn't turned my life over to Him. So I did it—that very night at the Crusade.' "[1]

Once again a man was forced to examine his soul.

I was in another country at one time and was invited to have lunch with a man who, materially speaking, had everything this world could offer. In fact, he expressed to me how he could buy anything he wanted. He had travelled extensively in business; everything he touched seemed to turn to gold. He was leader of his social set, and yet in his own words he said, "I'm a miserable old man, doomed to die. If there is a hell, that's where I'm headed."

I looked through the beautiful old windows at the snow falling gently on the manicured lawn and thought about others, like him, who had expressed to me similar thoughts about the emptiness of life without God—the meaninglessness of life for a man who has everything to live with, but nothing to live for. My attention came back with a start as I heard him say, "I've asked you here today to read the Bible to me and to talk to me about God. Do you think it's too late? My father and mother were strong believers in God and often prayed for me."

The verse from Matthew 4:4 flashed across my mind: "Man shall not live on bread alone." And Luke 12:15 tells us, "Not even when one has an abundance does his life consist of his possessions."

We read every day about the rich, the famous, the talented, who are disillusioned. Many of them are turning to the occult, or Transcendental Meditation, or Eastern religions. Some are turning to crime. The questions they thought were answered are left dangling: What is man? Where did he come from? What is his purpose on this planet? Where is he going? Is there a God who cares? If there is a God, has He revealed Himself to man?

Is the intellectual searching?

The men and women who are considered part of the intellectual community are searching for the same meaning, the same sense of fulfillment, but many are hampered by their own sense of pride. They would like to save themselves, because pride nourishes self-esteem, making us believe we can manage ourselves without God.

The famous English writer and philosopher Bertrand Russell wrote prolifically concerning ethics, morals, and human society, trying to prove what he believed were fallacies in the Bible. When it came to the pride of the intellectual, Russell wrote, "Every man would like to be God, if it were possible; some few find it difficult to admit the impossibility."[2]

From the beginning of time, man has said, like Lucifer, "I will be like the Most High" (Isa. 14:14, AV).

The search continues. The heart needs filling, and most intellectuals come to a point in their lives when the academe, the scientific community, the business or political activities are no longer enough.

A brilliant analyst of the cultural scene wrote: "Man, being human, however, tries again and again to evade the logic of his own position, and searches for his true self, his humanity, his freedom, even if he can only do so by means of sheer irrationality or completely unfounded mysticism."[3]

We see the results of man searching for his true self in mystic experiences, new cults, and what is called the New Consciousness. "Man today wants to experience God. It is not faith or knowledge which is the key word, but experience."[4]

As the desire for this experience increases, the false philosophies and false gods become acceptable. A European intellectual says: "For centuries there has been the search for the attainment of that ideal which the Greeks called ataraxia, the idea of quiet calm, of deep inner contentment, beyond the restlessness, frustrations, and tensions of normal living. Many searched for this via philosophy and religion, but always there has been the parallel search for short cuts."[5]

An American scholar writes, "As man's search for new experiences, new leaders, new hopes, increases in intensity, there will be that continued desire to find an alternative route into what appears to be a dark future."[6]

Men desperately want peace, but the peace of God is not absence from tension or turmoil, but peace in the midst of tension and turmoil.

In Calcutta, India, I wanted to see a great woman of God who is known to the world as Mother Theresa. I arrived early in the evening and the sisters hated to disturb Mother Theresa, because three men had died in her arms that day and she had just gone to her room to get a bit of rest. However, the official who brought me there sent a note to Mother Theresa, and in a few minutes she was there. I immediately had the impression of this saintly woman as a person who has peace in the midst of turmoil. It's the peace that passes all understanding, and all misunderstanding, too.

How desperately we need that kind of peace during a generation which is being torn apart by internal unrest and despair. The daily newspapers are classics in negative outlook. Terrorism, bombings, suicide, divorce, general pessimism are the diseases of the day because in his pride man refuses to turn to God!

The honest intellectual, however, the one who keeps an open mind along with his searching heart, is the one who makes a thrilling discovery. Dr. Rookmaaker says: "We cannot understand God fully, nor know His work completely. But we are not asked to accept in blind faith. On the contrary: we are asked to look around us, and know that the things He tells us through His Son and His prophets and apostles are true, real, and of this world, the cosmos He has made.

"Therefore our faith can never be just 'out of the box', irrational. Faith is not a sacrifice of the intellect if we believe in the biblical account of history."[7]

WHO NEEDS HELP?

In the rash of disaster movies in the middle 70s there was one called *Earthquake*. When the devastating quake hit, two of the main characters in the movie found shelter under a sturdy car from the flying debris and the terror of unleashed nature. At that moment they didn't reason about what had happened; they didn't analyse what they were going to do; they knew they needed help and dived for shelter.

The person who is on the bottom of life's circumstances wants help immediately. He doesn't need to analyse and examine how help comes; he only knows he needs to be saved.

When it comes to the disasters of our inner earthquakes some intellectuals want to know the source of help and all the details concerning that source. The intellectual has a certain set of beliefs which are self-sufficient and he believes his system is complete. Other intellectuals accept blindly the counterfeits which may be veiled in such complex language and thought patterns that the denial of their premises would sound ignorant. It's very difficult for some to say, "That doesn't really make good sense and I don't understand what is being said."

Nevertheless, many intellectual searchers have opened their minds and hearts to the truth of the Good News and found new life.

A young Hindu who was doing graduate study in nuclear medicine at UCLA was just beginning her second year of study when she came to a Crusade. At the end of the service she accepted Christ as her Saviour and was born again.

A brilliant surgeon who came to a Crusade heard me say that if gaining Heaven depended upon good deeds I wouldn't expect to get there. He had devoted his life to helping humanity, but at that moment he realised his training, his years of hard work and devotion, his sleepless nights with patients, and his love for his profession wouldn't earn him a place with God. This man, who had seen many births himself, knew what it was to be born twice.

Many people think Christ talked only to down-and-outers or children. One of His greatest encounteres during His teaching ministry was with an intellectual. This man, whose name was Nicodemus, had a very rigid philosophical and theological system, and it was a good plan, with God at the centre. However, this "intellectual" structured his philosophical religious system without the new birth—found only in Jesus Christ!

What did Jesus, the carpenter from Nazareth, tell this well-educated man? He said, in words like these, "Nicodemus, I'm sorry I can't explain to you. You have seen something that troubles you, that doesn't fit your system. You admit I am more than an ordinary man, that I act with the power of God. This may not make sense to you, but I can't explain it to you because your assumptions do not allow for a starting point. Nicodemus, to you it's not 'logical.' Nothing in your thought patterns permits it. You cannot see with spiritual insight until you are born spiritually. You will just have to be born again."

Nicodemus was baffled. " 'And how can a man who's getting old possibly be born?' replied Nicodemus. 'How can he go back into his mother's womb and be born for a second time?' " (John 3:4, Phillips).

The intellectual asks, "How can a man be born twice?"

If anyone is to find the answer to his search he must reject much of his old system and plunge into a new one. He will see the possibility of what he thought was impossible.

"That is also why only this uniquely 'impossible' faith—with a God who is, with an Incarnation that is earthly and historical, with a salvation that is at cross-purposes with human nature, with a Resurrection that blasts apart the finality of death—is able to provide an alternative to the sifting, settling dust of death and through a new birth open the way to new life."[8]

In the mountains near our home there was a small plane lost with four people on board. At the same time a fifteen-year-old girl was lost in approximately the same area in the Great Smoky Mountains. It was a sad time for our little community because the four were killed and the girl was never found.

As my wife talked about the tragic events of these people to a man who helps us, he told her a story from his own experience. He was born and raised in these mountains, he said, and thought he could never get lost. The mountains were his playground as a child and hunting area as an adult. One day, however, he found himself groping through the brush and clambering over the rocks, hopelessly confused. He wandered and retraced his steps and suddenly, to his relief, came upon an old man in a mountain cabin. He told Ruth that he would never forget the advice the old man gave him: "When you find yourself lost in the mountains, never go down—always go up. At the top of the ridge you can get your bearings and find your way again."

We can become lost in the mountain of life. We have two choices: we can either go down and get caught in drugs, depression, emptiness, and confusion, or we can keep heading up. The direction we go will determine whether we find ourselves or not.

In this Age of Quest the most important is our personal search for answers concerning life and about God. That search will propel us in the only true direction, in only one way, and we will be embarked on that journey when we are born again.

2

Can Anyone Tell Me Where to Find God?

A DRUNK WAS looking for something on the sidewalk one night under a street light. He groped along the ground, feeling the cement, occasionally grabbing the pole for support. A passerby asked what he was looking for. "Lost my wallet," the drunk replied. The passerby offered to help him look, but with no success.

"Are you sure you lost it here?" he asked the drunk.

" 'Course I didn't!" the drunk replied. "It was half a block back there."

"Then why aren't you looking back there?"

"Because," answered the drunk with baffling logic, "there ain't no street lights back there."

Searching is important, but it doesn't do any good unless we search in the right places.

The governor of one of our states entertained us in his home and after dinner asked to talk to me privately. We went into his study and I could see that he was struggling with his emotions, but finally he said, "I'm at the end of my rope, I need God. Can you tell me how to find Him?"

A young man, toughened in the Green Berets, so strong that his hands had been insured as lethal weapons, fell upon the floor of his room one night, weeping like a helpless child. "God, God, where are you?"

From the ghetto to the mansion, from community leader to prisoner on death row, man wonders if there is a God. And if there is, what is He like?

A remarkable fact for all seekers of God is that belief in some kind of God is practically universal. Whatever period of history we study, whatever culture we examine, if we look back in time we see all peoples, primitive or modern, acknowledging some kind of deity. During the past two centuries archaeology has unearthed the ruins of many ancient civilisations, but none has ever been found that did not yield some evidence of a god who was worshipped. Man has worshipped the sun and carved idols. Man has worshipped a set of rules, animals, and other men. Some seem to worship themselves. Man has made gods out of his imagination, although basically through a fog of confusion he believes that God does exist.

Some people give up the pursuit of God in frustration, calling themselves "atheists" or "agnostics," professing to be irreligious. Instead they find it necessary to fill the vacuum left within them with some other kind of deity. Therefore man makes his own "god"—money, work, success, fame, sex, or alcohol, even food.

Today many use their nation as an object of worship, espousing the gospel of nationalism. They mistakenly attempt to displace the true and living God with the religion of nationalism. Others make a god of their cause. Although many radical groups deny faith in God, thousands willingly lay down their lives and suffer privation and poverty because of their belief in "the cause" or "the revolution."

Failing to find the true God, millions declare their allegiance to lesser gods and causes. They find no ultimate answers or satisfaction, however. Just as Adam was made for fellowship with God, so are all men. Jesus commented on the First Commandment by saying, "And you shall love the Lord your God with all your heart, and with all your soul, and with all your mind, and with all your strength" (Mark 12:30).

He meant that man, unlike a stone or an animal, has the capacity to love God.

TWO-WAY SEARCH

Although the wise person seeks God, we have seen that he doesn't have the intellectual capacity to reason his way through to God. He must raise a serious personal question: "Is there any hope of being successful in this search? Can I really know God?"

Once when being interviewed by Ludovic Kennedy on BBC in London, I was asked, "Who made God?" The answer was simple. "No one made God." God is self-existent.

"In the beginning God" are the words which build the cornerstone of all existence. Without God there would have been no beginning and no continuing. God was the creating power and the cohesive force that brought cosmos out of chaos. By divine fiat He brought form out of shapelessness, order out of disorder, and light out of darkness.

Scientists cannot see God in a test tube or a telescope. God is God and the mind of man is too small!

Blaise Pascal, the celebrated seventeenth-century French physicist, said, "A unit joined to infinity adds nothing to it any more than one foot added to infinite length. The finite is swallowed up by the infinite and becomes pure zero. So are our minds before God."

As we seek this great God, what route are we to take? How can a created, finite human being, limited by time and space, understand an infinite God?

Our failure to comprehend God fully should not strike us as strange. After all, we live surrounded by mysteries we cannot explain——mysteries far simpler. Who can explain why objects are always attracted to the centre of the earth? Newton formulated the law of gravity, but he couldn't explain it. Who can explain reproduction? For years scientists have tried to reproduce a living cell and solve the mystery of procreation. They believe they are coming close, but as yet they are without success.

We have become accustomed to accepting as fact many mysteries we cannot explain. I am amazed when my wife mixes corn meal, shortening, eggs, baking powder, and buttermilk, and I see the soupy mixture slowly rise in the oven and come out light and fluffy with a crispy brown crust. I don't understand it, but I accept the results.

God is far more complex than some of the earthly phenomena we cannot understand. However, we could present many arguments before a very sceptical jury which would suggest the existence of God. In the scientific realm we know that whatever is in motion must be moved by something else, since motion is the response of matter to power. Yet in the world of matter there can be no power without life, and life presupposes a being who produces the power to move such things as tides and planets.

Another argument says that nothing can be the cause of itself. It would be prior to itself if it caused itself to be, and that is an absurdity!

Consider the law of life. We see objects that have no intellect, such as stars and planets, moving in a consistent pattern, cooperating ingeniously with one another. It is evident that they achieve their movements not by accident but by design.

Whatever lacks intelligence cannot move intelligently. What gives direction and design to these inanimate objects? It is God. He is the underlying, motivating force of life.

Many evidences and arguments suggest God's existence, yet the plain truth is that God cannot be proved by intellectual arguments alone. If the human mind could fully prove God, He would be no greater than the mind that proves Him!

Ultimately you must come to God by faith. Faith is the link

between God and man. The Scriptures say you must believe that *He is*. "Faith" is used many times in the Bible, and God has taken it upon Himself to encourage that faith. God continues to pursue man—just as man is searching for Him.

In spite of man's repeated rebellion. God loves man with an everlasting love. Some earthly fathers give up on their children when they fall into habits and company that are despicable. A father might order his son or daughter out of the house and tell them never to return. On the other hand, some fathers and even mothers deny their children before they are born. We know young people—even grown ones—whose lives are scarred by parental rejection. The only way such a person can be healed is to accept the fact and ask the Lord to supply the lack. The Bible says, "When my father and my mother forsake me, then the Lord will take me up" (Ps. 27:10, AV).

God has never forsaken man. The most dramatic quest of the centuries is God's loving and patient pursuit of man.

When man chose in the Garden of Eden to defy God's law, to break the line of communication between himself and God, they could no longer have fellowship. Light and darkness could not live side by side. Why did this barrier come between God and His creation? The cause is a characteristic of God that the average person does not comprehend. God is absolute "holiness."

Long ago God said to Israel, "I the Lord your God am holy" (Lev. 19:2).

In the Book of Revelation the cry in heaven night and day is, "HOLY, HOLY, HOLY, IS THE LORD GOD, THE ALMIGHTY, who was and who is and who is to come" (Rev. 4:8).

A holy God recoils from our evil; He cannot look upon sin because it is ugly and revolting to Him. Because man was stained with sin, God could no longer have fellowship with him. However, *God loves us—in spite of ourselves!*

God had a plan to restore fellowship with man, in spite of his sin. If God didn't have a plan, certainly no one else can! He had said to Adam and Eve at the very beginning when they broke His law, "You shall surely die" (Gen. 2:17). In a later chapter we will discuss the three dimensions of death. Man had to die or God would have had to go back on His word, and God cannot be a liar or He would no longer be God.

We can see that because man still sins, still defies authority and still acts independently of God, a great gulf exists between him and God. Twentieth-century man and woman are no different from Adam and Eve. We may have added some sophisticated technology, built a few skyscrapers, and written several million books, but there is still a chasm between sinful man and holy God. Yet across this dark, barren abyss, God calls, even pleads, with man to be reconciled to Him.

God loves us.

The Apostle John said that "God is love" (1 John 4:8).

The prophet Jeremiah quotes God as saying, " 'I have loved you with an everlasting love; therefore I have drawn you with lovingkindness' " (Jer. 31:3).

Another prophet, Malachi, said, " 'I have loved you,' says the Lord" (Mal. 1:2).

In every good novel or play there must be conflict. But even Shakespeare could not have created a more powerful plot than the divine dilemma. We know that man is sinful and separated from God. Because God is holy, He couldn't automatically forgive or ignore man's rebellion. Because God is love, He couldn't completely cast man aside. Conflict. How could God be just and the justifier? This is the question Job posed: "But how can a man be in the right before God?" (Job 9:2).

GOD SPEAKS

Radio was just coming of age when I was a boy. We would gather around a crude homemade set and twist the three tuning dials in an effort to establish contact with the transmitter. Often all the sound that came out of the amplifier was the squeak and squawk of static. It wasn't very exciting to listen to all those senseless sounds, but we kept at the controls with anticipation. We knew that somewhere out there was the unseen transmitter, so if contact was established and the dials were in adjustment we could hear a voice loud and clear. After a long time of laborious tuning the far distant sound of music or a voice would suddenly break through and a smile of triumph would brighten the faces of everyone in the room. At last we were tuned in!

Perhaps you have been puzzled that the prophets said God spoke to them. Does He speak to us? Does He tell us where He is—how we can find Him—how we can be right with Him? How God has answered these questions in His Word is the subject of part 2 of this book, which deals with the kind of person Jesus Christ was and the work He did. God has solved the problem; He does tell us about Himself and His loving concern. The key is a line of communication which is "revelation."

Revelation means "to make known" or "to unveil." Revelation requires a "revealer," who in this case is God. It also requires "hearers"—the chosen prophets and apostles who recorded in the Bible what He told them. Revelation is communication in which God is at one end and man is at the other.

In the revelation that God established between Himself and us we find a new dimension of living, but we must "tune in." Levels of living we have never attained await us. Peace, satisfaction, and joy we have never experienced are available to us. God is trying to break through. The heavens are calling and God is speaking!

Have you heard God's voice? At the same time you are searching for God, He is speaking to you.

3

Does God Really Speak to Us?

GOD HAS SPOKEN to us from the beginning. Adam heard the voice of the Lord in the Garden of Eden. God also spoke to Eve, and she knew who was speaking and must have trembled because she knew she had disobeyed Him.

Two people, a man and a woman, chose to disobey God and plunged into a world that was spiritually dark and dead—and physically unproductive except by hard work and suffering. The world was under the judgment of God. The Bible teaches that man is in a period of spiritual blackout. "The god of this world has blinded the minds of the unbelieving" (2 Cor. 4:4).

Isaiah, the great Hebrew prophet, said, "We grope along the wall like blind men, we grope like those who have no eyes; we stumble at midday as in the twilight, among those who are vigorous we are like dead men" (Isa. 59:10).

Isaiah was giving a vivid description of what sounds like physical blindness, but which is the darkness of the spirit.

To be trapped in physical darkness can be an uncanny

experience. When Cliff Barrows and I were in England just after World War II we drove down the streets in fog so thick that one of us had to walk in front of the car to prevent it from running into the kerb. This was a new experience, a type of "blackout" which was frightening.

How much worse it is to be forever spiritually blacked out and trapped! There are those who have physical blindness and yet are able to "see" better than a sighted person.

There is a beautiful Korean girl with a voice that has been described as "electric." She also plays the piano beautifully, and yet she is physically blind. Kim sees more than many with 20–20 vision and does not consider her blindness a handicap, but a gift from God. I have found her to have mental, psychological, and spiritual insights which are absolutely amazing.

Man is also spiritually deaf. Another great prophet said people have "ears to hear but do not hear" (Ezek. 12:2). Jesus said it with more force: "If they do not listen to Moses and the Prophets, neither will they be persuaded if someone rises from the dead" (Luke 16:31).

The difference between physical deafness and spiritual deafness is illustrated to me vividly at the Crusades. We have a section for the deaf and I have often stopped to shake hands with these men and women. At one Crusade about a dozen deaf persons were brought to see me in my office and I sat and talked to them through an interpreter. The light of Christ was quite obvious on the faces of many of them.

The world of the physically deaf is one which those of us with normal hearing find difficult to comprehend. But we walk in the world of the spiritually deaf every day.

Spiritually, many men and women are more than deaf and blind, they are dead. "You were dead in your trespasses and sins" (Eph. 2:1).

For the spiritually dead there is no communication with God. Millions of persons long for a world of joy, light, harmony, and peace; instead they are engulfed in a world of pessimism, darkness, discord, and turmoil. They search for happiness, but it eludes them, just as a sunbeam or a shaft of light eludes a child who tries to catch it.

Many give up and give in to pessimism. Often their despondent attitude leads to a circle of cocktail parties or bars where they obliterate the reality of their world with the unreality of alcohol. Sometimes they are led to drugs or an all-consuming pursuit of a hobby or a sport. All these are symptoms of the great escapist disease caused by an insidious infection called sin.

Many persons want to dissect God under their own microscopes. After establishing their own methods of analysis they come to no conclusions. God remains the great cosmic silence, unknown and unseen. However, God does communicate with those who are willing to obey him. He penetrates the dark silence with free, life-giving discoveries in nature, the human conscience, Scripture, and the Person of Jesus Christ.

GOD SPEAKS IN NATURE

I was present when our youngest son was born, and our three sons-in-law and our oldest son were present at the births of their children. We all felt that we had experienced a miracle. As one of the doctors said, "How can anyone deny the existence of God after witnessing birth?"

In its own language, nature speaks of God's existence, whether it is the cry of a baby or the song of a meadowlark. It is the language of order, beauty, perfection, and intelligence. The intricacies of a flower are God's work; the instincts of the birds are within His plans. God speaks in the regularity of the seasons; in the movements of the sun, moon, and stars; in the balance of the elements which allows us to breathe. "The heavens are telling of the glory of God; and the firmament is declaring the work of His hands. Day to day pours forth speech, and night to night reveals knowledge" (Ps. 19:1,2).

The very size of the universe has always been

incomprehensible to man, but as twentieth-century exploration has taken man into space our minds have become boggled. Every scientist who lacks belief in God must be completely baffled when he surveys how small man is on this earth—part of an estimated 100 billion galaxies, with 100 billion stars and planets in each galaxy.

With the exploration of the universe this generation has also looked at the other end of the scale. The electron microscope and biochemical research have enabled investigators to examine cells which have been magnified up to 200,000 times. There are so many molecules in one drop of water that if they could be transformed into grains of sand there would be enough sand to pave a road from Los Angeles to New York!

The Apostle Paul said, "For since the creation of the world His invisible attributes, His eternal power and divine nature, have been clearly seen, being understood through what has been made" (Rom. 1:20).

God says that we can learn a great deal about Him just by observing nature. Since He has spoken through His universe men and women are without excuse for not believing Him. This is the reason the Psalmist writes, "The fool has said in his heart, 'There is no God' " (Ps. 14:1).

God speaks in nature but we cannot know Him simply by sitting under a tree and gazing at the sky. He has another avenue of revelation for us which is often called that "still small voice."

GOD SPEAKS IN OUR CONSCIENCE

What is a conscience? A dictionary definition is "the sense of right and wrong; ideas and feelings within a person that tell him when he is doing right and warn him of what is wrong."

"Let your conscience be your guide" is sometimes wise advice, but not always. God shows Himself in our conscience. Sometimes it is a gentle teacher, prodding us in the right direction like the usher in a darkened theatre leading us to our seats. Other times our conscience is our worst enemy, torturing us day and night with agonising unrest.

Paul describes the working of conscience in this way: "For when Gentiles who do not have the Law do instinctively the things of the Law, these, not having the Law, are a law to themselves, in that they show the work of the Law written in their hearts, their conscience bearing witness, and their thoughts alternately accusing or else defending them" (Rom. 2:14,15).

"A man's conscience is the Lord's searchlight exposing his hidden motives" (Prov. 20:27, *The Living Bible*).

When we realise that God takes a powerful light and shines it into the darkest recesses of our minds, examining not just our actions, but the motives behind those actions, it becomes clear that God does indeed speak through our conscience.

Even people who are not Christians realise the existence of something within themselves which is a guiding force. Thomas Jefferson wrote almost two hundred years ago that "the moral sense, or conscience, is as much a part of man as his leg or arm. It is given to all human beings in a stronger or weaker degree, as force of members is given them in a greater or less degree."

Some persons, even without God, have a stronger sense of conscience than others. But the one with a seared or dead conscience is like an aeroplane without a pilot or a boat without a rudder—confused and directionless, on a collision course with circumstances. Through sin the conscience can become hardened, and even dead.

GOD SPEAKS IN SCRIPTURE

The Bible is the textbook of revelation. In God's great classroom there are three textbooks—one called nature, one called conscience, and one named Scripture. The laws God revealed in nature have never changed. In the written textbook of revelation—the Bible—God speaks through words. The Bible is the one book which reveals the Creator to the creature He created! No other book that man has conceived can make that statement and support it with fact.

The Bible is unique in its claims, its teachings, and its survival. Today there are many persons who are looking at books which are supposed to give the answers to the great questions of life and death; many of these books are products of Eastern religions or humanistic philosophy. In his book *Evidence That Demands a Verdict*, Josh McDowell quotes a former professor of Sanskrit who spent forty-two years studying Eastern books and said this in comparing them with the Bible: " 'Pile them, if you will, on the left side of your study table; but place your own Holy Bible on the right side—all by itself, all alone—and with a wide gap between them. For, ... there is a gulf between it and the so-called sacred books of the East which severs the one from the other utterly, hopelessly, and forever ... a veritable gulf which cannot be bridged over by any science of religious thought.' "[1]

Sceptics have attacked the Bible and retreated in confusion. Agnostics have scoffed at its teaching, but are unable to produce an intellectually honest refutation. Atheists have denied its validity, but must surrender to its historical accuracy and archaeological verification.

I picked up a reputable news magazine and read that a certain head of state made a remark about the economic trends. Nothing very startling about that. You and I read statements made by men and women every day. If we hear them from several different sources, we are inclined to believe that they're true and to tell someone else.

If we were confronted with a book which said in hundreds of different situations that, for instance, the Queen of England spoke, we would believe that she actually had been making statements. No doubt about it!

The writers of the Bible spoke in many ways to indicate that God gave them their information. In the Old Testament alone they said 3000 times that God spoke! Just in the first five books of the Bible we find such phrases as these:

"The Lord God called to the man"
"The Lord God said to the woman"
"The Lord said to Noah"
"God spoke unto Israel"
"God said"
"The Lord spoke saying"
"The Lord commanded"
"Hear the words of the Lord"
"Says the Lord"

Did God speak to these men as they were inspired to write? If He didn't, then they were the most blatant and consistent liars the world has even known, or they were mentally deranged. Would a variety of men from different areas, many of them not knowing each other, tell more than 3000 lies on one subject? If they were mistaken in this area why should we believe anything they said? If we cannot believe that God spoke to men in the Bible, then we cannot believe that the prophecies of these great men came true—and yet they did!

If someone lies to you two or three times, you begin to distrust him. You find it difficult, if not impossible, to believe anything he says. However, we would have to negate everything in the Bible if we thought that the Bible writers lied when they said God spoke.

Jesus quoted frequently from the Old Testament. He knew it well and never doubted the Scriptures. He said, "Scripture cannot be broken" (John 10:35).

The Apostles often quoted the Old Testament Scriptures. Paul said, "All Scripture is inspired by God" (2 Tim. 3:16). Peter said, "For no prophecy was ever made by an act of human will, but men moved by the Holy Spirit spoke from God" (2 Pet. 1:21).

Many people get their belief about the Bible from secondhand sources. A smattering of biblical movie epics, some television reruns, hearsay, and courses on comparative religion give them man's view of Scripture. In high school or college classes students take courses in "The Bible as Literature." Many times these classes are used to undermine the faith of young people unless there is a teacher who understands the Bible and has a strong faith in God. I know students who have studied such topics as "The Myths and Discrepancies of the Bible."

Secondhand sources will not do.

A verse or a story in the Bible may speak to someone in a way someone else could not imagine. It was a firsthand source in a secondhand bookstore that changed the lives of an entire family.

My wife has a weakness for books—especially old, choice religious books which are now out of print. At one time Foyles in London had a large secondhand religious book department. One day during the 1954 London Crusade she was browsing through the books in Foyles when a very agitated clerk popped out from behind the stacks and asked if she was Mrs. Graham. When she told him that she was, he began to tell her a story of confusion, despair, and frustration. His marriage was on the rocks, his home was breaking up, and business problems were mounting. He explained that he had explored every avenue for help and as a last resort planned to attend the services at Harringay arena that night. Ruth assured him that she would pray for him, and she did. That was in 1954.

In 1955 we returned to London. Again my wife went into Foyles' secondhand book department. This time the same clerk appeared from behind the stacks, his face wreathed in smiles. After expressing how happy he was to see her again, he explained that he had gone to Harringay that night in 1954 as he had said he would, that he had found the Saviour, and that the problems in his life had sorted themselves out.

Then he asked Ruth if she would be interested in knowing what verse it was that "spoke to him." She was. Again he disappeared behind all the books and reappeared with a worn Bible in his hand. He turned to Psalm 102, which I had read the night that he had attended the Crusade. He pointed out verse 6, "I am like a pelican of the wilderness; I am like an owl of the desert" (AV). This had so perfectly described to him his condition that he realised for the first time how completely God understood and cared. As a result he was soundly converted to the Lord Jesus Christ. And subsequently so was his entire family.

My wife was in London during 1972 at the time of a Harringay reunion. As the ceremonies closed, a gentleman came up to speak to her, but he didn't have to introduce himself. She recognised the clerk from Foyles. He was radiantly happy, introduced his Christian family, and explained how they were all now in the Lord's work—all because God spoke to him when he was "an owl of the desert"!

Make use of this tool of communication by which God speaks to us—namely, the Bible! Read it, study it, memorise it. It will change your entire life. It is not like any other book. It is a "living" book that works its way into your heart, mind and soul.

SPEAKING IN DARK PLACES

In places where there is easy accessibility to the Bible, it may gather dust on the shelf. In countries where the Bible is subversive literature, God speaks in unusual ways.

A famous violinist was invited years ago by Chou En-lai to teach at one of the famous universities in the People's Republic of China. He was told that if he wanted to leave he would be able to do so. After seven years this violonist was completely disillusioned.

When he went to the exit permit office to apply for the right to leave, he was refused. However, he returned every day, and one day a piece of paper was slipped into his pocket. On returning home he found it there and pulled it out, only to discover that it was a page from the Bible. He read it with interest and found that it strangely spoke to his heart. On one of his subsequent visits a man came up to him and asked if he would like another page from the Bible. He said he would.

Each day when he returned to the exit permit office he was

supplied with another page from the Bible. There in the People's Republic of China he was soundly converted to Jesus Christ. Ultimately he received his exit permit and went to Hong Kong. He is now a professor in another country.

When Corrie ten Boom was in Ravensbruck prison camp it was the studying and teaching of the Word of God which kept her mind clear so that when she was released she was mentally alert. Many inmates upon their release were little more than vegetables and had to be cared for until they regained some form of normalcy.

A similar story is told of a missionary who was imprisoned by the Japanese in China. At this concentration camp the penalty for owning even a portion of the Scriptures was death. However, a small Gospel of John was smuggled to her in a winter coat. At night when she went to bed she pulled the covers over her head and with her flashlight read a verse and then put herself to sleep memorising that verse. In this way, over a period of time, she memorised the entire Gospel of John.

When she went to wash her hands she would take one page at a time, dissolve it in the soap and water, and flush it down the drain. "And that is the way," she said, "that John and I parted company."

This little missionary was interviewed by a *Time* reporter just before the prisoners were released. The reporter happened to be standing at the gates when the prisoners came out. Most of them shuffled along, eyes on the ground, little more than automatons. Then out came the little missionary, bright as a button. One of the reporters was heard to ask, "I wonder if they managed to brainwash her?"

The *Time* reporter overheard the remark and said, "God washed her brain!"

The Word of God hidden in the heart is a stubborn voice to suppress. Ruth had another experience in London which emphasises this fact. During the meetings in Earls Court in 1966 she made friends with a little Cockney beatnik. Each night as we arrived, this thoroughly likable. irrepressible little rebel would be waiting for Ruth. During the Earls Court Crusade she would frequently sit with Ruth. or sometimes just walk with her to her seat. They began an unusual, but lasting friendship.

Ruth learned that the girl had, previous to her conversion, been on drugs. Ruth told her to memorise several verses which she felt would be important to her, like John 3:16, 1 John 1:8, and the last two verses of Jude. One night she even warned her that, because of her past background, when she hit a snag in life she would have two choices: one was to go back on drugs, the other was to go forward with the Lord Jesus Christ.

One night during the service the usher gave my wife a note saying, "I am on drugs and I need you. Please come help me." It was signed by this young friend.

Ruth slipped out of the meeting and found her waiting—white-faced, hollow-eyed. and obviously drugged. Ruth, having had little previous experience with drug-users, thought that they were handled as drunks and took her to a coffee stand to get her a cup of coffee. She didn't realise that was the last thing she should have done. On the way she asked the girl why she had done this, only to receive the reply. "Me best friend died on an overdose today."

Ruth wanted her to hear the sermon, and they sat down on a step within earshot of the service. The girl was in no condition to hear. Realising that her little friend was fast passing out, Ruth wrote on the little card found at the bottom of a pocket package of Kleenex, something to this effect: "God loves me. Jesus died for me. No matter what I have done, He will forgive me if I repent and ask Him to forgive me."

The following year, 1967. we were back in London at Earls Court for another series of meetings. One evening Ruth was having tea with her young beatnik friend. The girl fished into her sack and brought out the crumpled Kleenex card on which Ruth had written the words the previous year. She asked Ruth when she had written these words. Ruth told her, but the girl had no recollection of what had happened that night. Then she repeated the verses of Scripture that Ruth told her to learn and asked when it was that she had learned them. Ruth explained to her, but she didn't remember the occasion. It is interesting that the drugs could cause amnesia up to a certain point, but they had not been able to take away the Word of God which she had hidden away in her heart.

A similar situation happened when Ruth fell out of a tree while trying to build a pipeslide for our grandchildren. She suffered a severe concussion and was unconscious for the better part of a week. As she regained consciousness, the thing that concerned her the most was that she could remember so little. Her greatest loss was that of the Bible verses which she had memorised down through the years.

In her notebook she has written how one night as she was fuzzily praying about this fact, out of nowhere came the words, "I have loved thee with an everlasting love, therefore with loving kindness have I drawn thee." There was no recollection of when or where she had memorised the verse, for her mind was still foggy. And yet—there it was!

GOD SPEAKS IN JESUS CHRIST

God speaks most clearly in the person of His Son Jesus Christ. "God, ... in these last days has spoken to us in His Son" (Heb. 1:1,2).

Throughout the ages many people have believed that God is a spirit within everyone. Tolstoi, the great Russian writer, said, "Every man recognises within himself a free and rational spirit, independent of his body. This spirit is what we call God."

Philosophers have found God in everything. In the first century the Roman philosopher Seneca set the stage for belief throughout the ages when he wrote, "Call it nature, fate, fortune: all are but names of the one and same God."

Seneca was, of course, wrong. But so have millions of men throughout the ages been equally mistaken.

In most religions of the world we find some references to a belief that God would visit the earth. There have been many men who have come claiming they are God. One man from Korea during our time has drawn many followers by claiming to be the "Lord of the Second Advent."

However, it was not until the "fullness of time" when all the conditions were right, when all the prophecies were fulfilled, that God "sent forth His Son, born of a woman" (Gal. 4:4).

In a little town in the Middle East almost 2000 years ago, the prophecy in Micah 5:2 was fulfilled when God "was revealed in the flesh" (1 Tim. 3:16). This revelation came in the person of Jesus Christ.

The Scripture says about Christ, "In Him all the fullness of Deity dwells in bodily form" (Col. 2:9).

This revelation is the most complete God ever gave to the world. Do you want to know what God is like? All you have to do is look at Jesus Christ.

Nature has perfection and beauty; we see order, power, and majesty in the physical world around us. All of these descriptions apply to Jesus Christ. In the working of our conscience and the magnificence of the written Scriptures we find justice, mercy, grace and love. These are attributes of Jesus Christ. "The Word [logos] became flesh, and dwelt among us" (John 1:14).

To His disciples and to all of us living in this twentieth-century world, Jesus said, "Believe in God, believe also in Me" (John 14:1). This sequence of faith is inevitable. If we believe in what God made and what God said, we must believe in the One whom God sent.

How can we believe? The means of understanding these facts of salvation is "faith." We are not always challenged to understand everything, but we are told to believe. "But these have been written that you may believe that Jesus is the Christ, the Son of God; and that believing you may have life in His name" (John 20:31).

Every need to know God, every expectation of eternal life,

every desire for a new social order—all must be tied to the only One who can accomplish these goals—Jesus Christ. When we come to Jesus Christ, the unknown becomes known; we experience God Himself.

When our groping, darkened lives experience the light of the eternal presence of God, we are able to see that another world stretches beyond the confusion and frustration of the world we live in.

A small child, not even old enough for school, went into one of those mirrored mazes at an amusement park. When her father discovered that she had slipped away he saw her trying to find her way out and beginning to cry in fear. She became increasingly confused by all the paths, until she heard her daddy call out, "Don't cry, darling. Put your hands out and reach all around. You'll find the door. Just follow my voice."

As he spoke the little girl became calm and soon found her way out and ran to the security of her father's outstretched arms.

God has revealed Himself to the human race on this little planet through nature, conscience, the Bible—and fully in the person of Jesus Christ.

4

But I'm Not Religious!

THE QUESTION IS often heard, "What about all the other religions of the world? Isn't one religion just as good as another?"

Few terms in the language of man have been so distorted and misunderstood as that of "religion." The eighteenth-century German philosopher Immanuel Kant described religion as "morality or moral action." Hegel, one philosopher who influenced Hitler's thinking, said religion was "a kind of knowing."

"Religion" has many meanings for many people. It can mean the sadistic symbolism of the Manson girls, who cut an "x" on their foreheads; it can be the rituals of Transcendental Meditation or the chants of various cults; or it can suggest quiet meditation within the comforting walls of a church.

Many people say rather proudly, "I'm not very religious," but in spite of some of his own objections man is a religious being. The Bible, anthropology, sociology, and other sciences teach us that people long for some sort of religious experience.

My major in college was anthropology, which the dictionary explains as a science dealing with the races, customs, and beliefs of mankind. I have also had the privilege of travelling extensively on every continent. I have found from personal experience that what I learned from anthropology is true: man has naturally and universally a capacity for religion—and not only a capacity, for the vast majority of the human race practices or professes some form of religion.

Religion can be defined as having two magnetic poles, the biblical and the naturalistic. The biblical pole is described in the teachings of the Bible. The naturalistic pole is explained in all the man-made religions. In humanistic systems there are always certain elements of truth. Many of these faiths have borrowed from Judeo-christianity; many use portions and incorporate their own fables. Other religions or faiths have in fragments what Christianity has as a whole.

The Apostle Paul described the naturalistic pole when he said that men "exchanged the glory of the incorruptible God for an image in the form of corruptible man and of birds and four-footed animals and crawling creatures" (Rom. 1:23).

All false religions cut away parts of God's revelation, add ideas of their own, and come out with various viewpoints that differ from God's revelation in the Bible. Natural religion does not come from God, but from the natural world He created and that turned away from Him in its pride.

A false religion is like the imitation of high fashion. I've read that after an exclusive showing of original designs in one of the fashion centres of the world like Paris, copies will soon appear in the mass merchandising stores under different labels. The very presence of counterfeits proves the existence of the real. There would be no imitations without a genuine product.

God's original design has always had imitators and counterfeits!

THE BIRTH OF RELIGION

How did all the religions of the world get started? A famous military conqueror from the past was able to state a truth, without realising that he had charged right past the real Truth. Napoleon Bonaparte stated, "I would believe in a religion if it existed ever since the beginning of time, but when I consider Socrates, Plato, Muhammad, I no longer believe. All religions have been made by man."

John Bunyan once said, "Religion is the best armour that a man can have, but it's the worst cloak."

When did man invent this maze of religion? It began with a couple of fellows who are rather well known. When Adam and Eve had their sons, we might have thought they would have been able to instill in both of them the importance of a right relationship with God. However, Cain wanted to do it his own way. He approached the first altar with his offering of "the fruit of the ground," trying to regain "paradise" without accepting God's plan of redemption. Cain brought what he had grown, the distinctive elements of his own culture. Today we would call Cain's gift his attempt at salvation by works. But God never said we could work our way to heaven.

His brother, Abel, obeyed God and humbly offered the first of his flock in a sacrifice of blood. Abel agreed with God that sin deserved death and could be covered before God only through the substitutionary death of a guiltless sacrifice. Cain deliberately rejected this plan. God demanded a blood sacrifice.

The Bible writers knew that blood was absolutely essential for life. A person or an animal might get along without a leg or an eye, but no animal or man could live without blood. That is why the Old Testament said, "For the life of the flesh is in the blood" (Lev. 17:11).

Thus, the Bible teaches that atonement for sin comes only through the shedding of blood. "In fact, the law requires that nearly everything be cleansed with blood, and without the shedding of blood there is no forgiveness" (Heb. 9:22, NIV).

When we speak of the blood of Christ, therefore, we are saying that He died for us. Blood sacrifice underlined the seriousness of sin. Sin was a life-and-death matter. Only the shedding of blood could atone for sin. The death of Christ also underlined the principle of substitution. In the Old Testament a sacrificed animal was seen as a substitute; the innocent animal took the place of the guilty person. In the same way, Christ died in our place. He was innocent, but He freely shed His blood for us and took our place. We deserved to die for our sins, but He died in our place.

Because of Christ's death for us, we can know His life—now and eternally. "Knowing that you were not redeemed with perishable things ... but with precious blood ... of Christ" (1 Pet. 1:18,19).

When Cain chose to go his way, not God's way of blood, something bitter happened to his heart. He began to hate his brother Abel. Just as the true Christian believer will often not be accepted by those who have their man-made religion, Abel was not accepted by Cain, and this hatred festered until Cain killed his brother.

Pride, jealousy, and hatred have been in the human heart in all cultures and all ages. Many years ago when I was a student in Florida a young man killed his older brother in a fit of jealousy. His father and mother had both been killed in an automobile crash, and when the will was read it indicated that the older brother had received two-thirds of an orange grove, leaving only a third to the younger brother. He became moody and depressed, angry at his deceased parents, and intensely jealous of his brother. Then the older brother disappeared, and about six weeks later his body was found tied with wire to the trunk of a cypress tree in a river.

Times haven't changed. Millions want salvation, but on their own terms; they want to chart their own courses and devise all kinds of routes to lead to God.

If Christianity is true, it is not a religion. Religion is man's effort to reach God. The dictionary describes religion as a "belief in God or gods ... or worship of God or gods." Religion can be anything! But true Christianity is God coming to man in a personal relationship.

The modern interest in the occult and in Eastern religions is indicative of man's eternal search for God. We cannot escape the fact that man is instinctively religious, but God has chosen to reveal Himself to us through nature, conscience, the Scriptures, and through Jesus Christ. The Scripture says there is no excuse for a person not to know God!

IN THE NAME OF "RELIGION"

It's no wonder that people say with satisfaction, "I'm not religious." Extreme cruelties and great injustices have been perpetrated in the name of religion.

In China when my wife was growing up, frequently babies who died before cutting their teeth were thrown out to be eaten by pariah dogs. The people feared that if evil spirits thought they cared too much for the children they would come and take another one. They tried to prove their indifference in this crude way. "Religion" impressed Ruth as being grim and joyless, and often cruel.

I once saw a man in India lying on a bed of spikes. He had been there for many days, eating no food and drinking little water. He was attempting to atone for his sins. Another time in Africa I saw a man walk on coals of fire. Supposedly, if he came through unscathed, he was accepted by God; if he was burned, he was considered to be a sinner in need of more repentance.

In India a missionary who passed the banks of the Ganges noticed a mother sitting by the river bank with two of her children. On her lap was a beautiful new baby and whimpering beside her was a painfully retarded child of about three. On her return home that night, the missionary saw the young mother still sitting at the river bank, but the baby was gone and the mother was trying to comfort her little retarded child. Horrified at what she thought might be true, the missionary hesitated a moment and then walked over to the mother and asked her what had happened. With tears streaming down her cheeks, the mother looked up and said "I don't know about the god in your country, but the god in mine demands the best." She had given her perfect baby to the god of the Ganges.

People have made human sacrifices in the name of religion. They have worshipped all types of idols, from brass monkeys to trees. In some of the Pacific islands, for instance, some of the islanders believe that the souls of their ancestors are in certain trees. Offerings are made to the tree, and they believe that if any injury occurs to the tree, some misfortune will come upon the village. They fear that if the tree were cut down, the village and all its inhabitants would inevitably perish.

In the name of religion, kings, emperors, and leaders of nations and tribes have been worshipped as gods. One English scholar wrote, "At a certain stage of early society the king or priest is often thought to be endowed with supernatural powers or to be an incarnation of a deity; ... he is held responsible for bad weather, failure of the crops, and similar calamities."[1]

An example of the class of monarchs worshipped as deity is the Mikado, the spiritual emperor of Japan. In an official decree he received the title of "manifest or incarnate deity." An early account says of the Mikado: "It was considered as a shameful degradation for him even to touch the ground with his foot.... None of the superfluities of the body were ever taken from him, neither his hair, his beard, nor his nails were cut."[2]

Many people will shrug at "religion" and agree with the philosophy professor from a prestigious American university who wrote: "The term 'religion' has come into use as a label for referring all at once to Judaism, Christianity, Islam, Buddhism, Hinduism, Taoism, and Confucianism, as well as a great many other siblings, some of whom have proper names and some of whom do not, but all of whom are taken to be sufficiently similar to the seven mentioned here to make it useful to lump them together."[3]

Can we really lump Christianity with every "religion" of the world?

WITHOUT EXCUSE

From the very beginning of time, "natural" religion was introduced onto the human stage as a substitute for God's plan. The Apostle Paul describes this phenomenon in his letter to the Romans, using references to images resembling birds, animals, and serpents to illustrate man-made religion. But this doesn't describe all its forms. Today there are many new and more sophisticated religious expressions—especially at some universities—but they are really from the same root: man seeking God consciously or unconsciously.

Paul describes man's corruption of God's revelation: "For since the creation of the world His invisible attributes, His eternal power and divine nature, have been clearly seen, being understood through what has been made, so that they are without excuse. For even though they knew God, they did not honour Him as God, or give thanks; but they became futile in their speculations, and their foolish heart was darkened. Professing to be wise, they became fools .... For they exchanged the truth of God for a lie, and worshipped and served the creature rather than the Creator, who is blessed forever" (Rom. 1:20–25).

Paul is simply saying that all men everywhere possess at least a primitive knowledge of God. Some people greet this idea with cynicism, which initiates the inevitable question: What about the pagans who have never heard of Jesus?

What about the pagans on Main Street, U.S.A., or the pagans at Oxford or the Sorbonne? God created all of us in His image; everyone is answerable to the light that He revealed to them. How can a just God condemn people who have never had the opportunity of hearing the gospel? The answer is in Genesis 18:25: "Shall not the Judge of all the earth do right?" (AV).

God's nature will bear witness of a divine power and person to whom everyone will answer. On the other side, God's justice will be exhibited against those who fail to live up to the light that He has given them.

In my lifetime, I have heard of many instances in which people have been given insight into the "eternal power and divine nature" of God, without benefit of a Bible or an evangelistic crusade.

In the middle 1950s, we held a major Crusade in Madras, India. One man walked over 120 miles to attend these meetings. I was told that this man came from a village that had never had a missionary and, so far as anyone knew, the gospel of Christ was completely unknown. Yet he longed with all his heart to know the true and living God. He heard that a "guru" from America was going to be speaking, and his desire for God was so intense that he came and found Christ. Eight months later when Bishop Newbigin of the Church of South India (who told me the story) visited the village, he found the entire community had been turned into a church. Everyone had been led to Christ by this one man.

When we were preaching in north-east India in 1972, people walked for as much as ten days, carrying all their belongings on their shoulders, bringing their entire families from such places as Nepal, Sikkim, and Burma. We were told that a number of those people had never heard the name of Jesus Christ. They just heard that a religious meeting was going to be held and they wanted to come and see what it was about. Many stayed to find Christ.

I am convinced that when a man sincerely searches for God with all his heart, God will reveal Himself in some way. A person, a Bible, or some experience with believers will be used by God to reach the one who seeks.

A famous Bible teacher, Dr. Donald Barnhouse, told about a boat trip he had to take through the middle of Africa on a river. When he got into the boat, he noticed a chicken and thought it was probably for their next meal. After two or three hours he heard a roar in the distance and realised that they were approaching very turbulent water. The nationals who were rowing the boat steered it over to the bank, got out, and took the chicken into the woods. There they made a very crude altar. Preparatory to sacrificing the chicken, they chopped off its head and sprinkled the blood over the front of the boat. Dr. Barnhouse said he realised once more that even without a missionary and without God's Word having been taught to those people, they knew a sacrifice was necessary.

So Paul says that God has seen to it that all people everywhere possess basic knowledge of Him, His attributes, power, and divine nature. Through what they can observe, and through their consciences, they can respond to Him if they wish.

But humankind has turned away from Him. Their minds did not love the truth enough, their wills didn't desire to obey Him, their emotions were not excited by the prospect of pleasing Him.

What happened? What is still happening? Man suppresses the truth, mixes it with error, and develops the religions of the world.

Humanistic religions are often offended by biblical faith, which is the belief that accepts the Bible as the authoritative source of what sin is, and how through the life and atoning death of Christ, God can declare sinners "just." Natural religion contains just enough truth to make it deceptive. It may contain elements of the truth, or high ethical standards. Some of its followers at times use terms which sound like the language of the Bible. The English scholar C. S. Lewis said that all religions are really a preview or a perversion of Christianity.

Religion of man may have a very pleasant sound. Thomas Paine wrote, "The world is my country, all mankind are my brethren, and to do good is my religion." While morality or "do-goodness" may win the approval of men, it is not acceptable to God, nor does it reflect His full moral demands. In fact, some of the crudest immorality in human history has had the approval of natural religion.

There is a great counterfeiter who adapts himself to every culture, even deceiving true believers at times. He doesn't charge on the scene clothed in red and wearing a hideous mask but charms his way as an "angel of light." This is how Satan operates. Thousands of people have entered churches without discovering a vital experience with Jesus Christ. The substitutes have been handed them in the guise of religious rituals, good works, community effort, or social reform, all of which are commendable actions in themselves, but none of which can gain a person a right relationship with God.

There are many people who say, "I guess I'm a Christian," or "I try to be a Christian." There's no guess or "try to" in the Christian life. Even some of the great intellects of our time have not come to grips with this truth: The simplicity of the gospel can reach the mentally retarded as well as the geniuses.

THE COMPROMISERS

Where there is truth and error there is always compromise. Within some churches there is a movement to reshape the Christian message to make it more acceptable to modern man. A view held by many is that "the Christian churches have been, and still are, fountainheads of anti-intellectualism and opposition to critical thinking."[4]

Books are written and sermons preached scoffing at the Bible and the basic beliefs of the Christian faith. One thick volume is called *Bible Myths* and the chapter titled "The Miracles of Christ" starts this way: "The legendary history of Jesus of Nazareth, contained in the books of the New Testament, is full of prodigies and wonders. These alleged prodigies, and the faith which the people seem to have put in such a tissue of falsehoods, indicate the prevalent disposition of the people to believe in everything, and it was among such a class that Christianity was propagated."[5]

Time magazine, in a lengthy article on the Bible, said, "Questions about the Bible's truth are nothing new; they have arisen from its earliest days."[6]

There was an archaeology professor I knew at Wheaton College who was also studying at the University of Chicago. Frequently his Chicago professor would bring up some point to undermine the trustworthiness of the Scriptures. On each occasion the archaeology teacher would bring out some archaeological find which proved the authenticity of the Scriptures. At one point that professor at the University of Chicago exclaimed in exasperation, "That's the trouble with you evangelical archaeologists! You're always digging up something to prove us wrong and the Bible right!"

Archaeology has never uncovered anything that disproved the Scriptures.

Among the compromisers are theologians who fail to agree among themselves on which part of the New Testament to retain and which part to reject. Some of them seem to agree that the miracles were myths. They regard the resurrection as a subjective experience of the disciples rather than an objective historical event. They question that Jesus Christ was supernatural and reject any explanation that says part of His excellence came from the fact that He was God as well as man.

C. S. Lewis was baffled by biblical critics who would pick and choose among the supernatural events they accepted. "He wondered at the selective theology of the Christian exegete who, 'after swallowing the camel of Resurrection, strains at such gnats as the feeding of the multitudes.' "[7]

THE DECEIVERS

From compromise to deceit is a small step. All through the Bible we are warned about false prophets and false teachers. Jesus said, "Beware of the false prophets, who come to you in sheep's clothing, but inwardly are ravenous wolves .... So then, you will know them by their fruits" (Matt. 7:15,20).

Sometimes the "sheep's clothing" is a clergyman's robe. He

may be a liberal or a fundamentalist. The liberal is like the Sadducees of old, denying biblical truth. The extreme fundamentalists, like the Pharisees of old, may accept sound theology but add so much nonbiblical material to it. Other times the clothing may be worn by someone with a string of degrees, who speaks with logical-sounding phrases. It's difficult sometimes for a Christian to discern a false teacher, since in some ways he resembles the true teacher. Jesus spoke of false prophets who "show great signs and wonders, so as to mislead, if possible, even the elect" (Matt. 24:24).

The person behind the Great Deception is Satan himself. He is crafty and clever, working in such subtle and secretive ways that no Christian should brag that he is beyond the assaults of Satan.

The Apostle Paul warned Timothy, "But evil men and impostors will proceed from bad to worse, deceiving and being deceived" (2 Tim. 3:13). He also warned the church at Ephesus, "Let no one deceive you with empty words" (Eph. 5:6); and again, "As a result, we are no longer to be children, tossed here and there by waves, and carried about by every wind of doctrine, by the trickery of men, by craftiness in deceitful scheming" (Eph. 4:14).

A woman who now leads hundreds of women each week in a Bible class in California said that for years her pseudo-intellectualism had her grabbing onto every "religious thought" that was presented. After accepting Jesus Christ as her Saviour and being born again spiritually, she said, "I'm no longer a child … carried about by every wind of doctrine."

This is a time when more false teachers will appear. We may be living in a time in history when this age may be drawing to an end. The Apostle Peter said: "But false prophets also arose among the people, just as there will also be false teachers among you, who will secretly introduce destructive heresies, even denying the Master who bought them, bringing swift destruction upon themselves. And many will follow their sensuality, and because of them the way of the truth will be maligned; and in their greed they will exploit you with false words; and their judgment from long ago is not idle, and their destruction is not asleep" (2 Pet. 2:1-3).

When we realise that the heresies and the deceptions are secretly introduced, it should make us even more alert. The Sunday school, the Bible class, the pulpit, the classroom, and the mass media are being invaded en masse. Some of the terms of Christianity are even being used, for example, *peace, love, born again*. Watch for the words which pepper secular literature and have entirely different meanings: *messiah, a christ, redemption, regenerate, genesis, conversion, mercy, salvation, apostle, prophet, deliverer, saviour, a spiritual leader*. Even great theological terms like *evangelical, infallible Bible*, etc., are rapidly losing their former meaning.

Thousands of untaught Christians are being deceived today, as are millions of people who are rejecting or ignoring the true Christ. Deceivers with intellectual arguments which sound like the epitome of scholarship are beguiling many.

Paul is not gentle with the false teachers. He says, "But the Spirit explicitly says that in later times some will fall away from the faith, paying attention to deceitful spirits and doctrines of demons, by means of the hypocrisy of liars' (1 Tim. 4:1,2).

The Bible is very clear that many have turned away because they listened to Satan's lies and deliberately chose to accept the doctrines of devils rather than the truth of God.

BACK TO BASICS

Church members and spiritually thirsty non-church members have been hungry for a personal, vital experience with Jesus Christ. Many have been turning to other forms of worship in addition to the church service.

In 1965 I wrote in my book *World Aflame* that "unless the church quickly recovers the authoritative biblical message, we may witness the spectacle of millions of Christians going outside the institutional church to find spiritual food." This is exactly what has happened.

We now estimate that there are over two million prayer groups and Bible study groups meeting in homes and churches in the United States that were not meeting ten years ago. One of the great hopes we see is that denominational leadership is beginning to recognise this and promote Bible studies conducted on a lay level with adequate leadership.

Our own Crusade preparation has revealed in recent years a far greater increase in actual home prayer meeting groups. In our most recent Crusades we established a prayer group on every block in the city. The result is that thousands of additional prayer meeting groups are being held in connection with the Crusades— in some cities as many as 5,000.

With nearly 50 million adult Americans having experienced "born again" religious conversions, I believe it is important to have a clear understanding of what this is all about.

AN OLD CLICHE

Nothing could be more grossly wrong than the old cliché that "any religion will do, as long as you're sincere." What if the same line of reasoning were used with a baby? The mother would say, "I don't have any milk, but I truly want my baby to be fed, so I'll just put some Coke or a little wine in the bottle. After all, they're all liquids." Ridiculous as that may sound, it is no more so than the old "sincerity" answer.

Who invented religion? Let's go back to the brothers again. The two altar fires outside Eden illustrate the difference between true and false religion. One belonged to Abel, who made an offering to the Lord God from the first-born of his flock. Abel acted in love, adoration, humility, reverence, and obedience. And the Bible says that the Lord held Abel and his offering in high regard.

His older brother, Cain, brought a bloodless, cheap offering to the altar, and the Bible says of God that "for Cain and for his offering He had no regard" (Gen. 4:5).

Was God being unfair? After all, didn't Cain attempt to please God? Wasn't he sincere?

This story was put in the Bible to teach us there is a right way and a wrong way to make contact with God. Abel brought a sacrifice of blood as God had instructed; Cain made his vegetable sacrifice selfishly and superficially, disobeying God by coming without faith. When God didn't bless his sacrifice, Cain killed his brother. Cain's worship was empty religiosity, hollow as his whole life became. He left his family and walked the earth as a bitter man, crying out to the Lord, "My punishment is too great to bear" (Gen. 4:13).

Cain was sincere—but wrong.

Humanistic religion emerges under the very noses of great men of God. While Moses was on Mount Sinai receiving the tablets of stone "written with the finger of God," false religion was erupting in the camp of Israel. The people said to Aaron, "Come, make us a god who will go before us." Aaron was carried along with the idea of a new religion and said, "Tear off the gold rings which are in the ears of your wives, your sons, and your daughters, and bring them to me." Out of this gold he made a molten calf and the people said, "This is your god, O Israel, who brought you up from the land of Egypt" (Exod. 32:1–4).

Throughout time other idolatrous beliefs have eroded the foundations of truth. Whether ancient or modern, all have posed alternatives to the biblical way of approaching God.

Men and women may devise plans to satisfy their inner longings, but in the midst of all the "religions" of the world God's way is available in the Bible for all who will come to Him on His terms.

For the person who searches, the answers are available.

5

What Is This Thing Called Sin?

THERE'S A STORY about a jet which was travelling from Chicago to Los Angeles. As the gigantic plane levelled out at 40,000 feet, the passengers heard a voice over the loudspeaker.

"This is a recording. You have the privilege of being the first to fly in a wholly electronic jet. This plane took off electronically. It is now flying at 40,000 feet electronically. It will land in Los Angeles electronically.

"This plane has no pilot, no co-pilot, no flight engineer. But don't worry. Nothing can go wrong ... go wrong ... go wrong ... go wrong ... go wrong ... "

Something has gone wrong with our jet age. It's supposed to be scientifically sophisticated and morally liberated. But it isn't. What's gone wrong?

In every major city in America and Europe crime is up. The crime wave has hit the world with hurricane force. A news magazine reported that in the U.S. "in the past 14 years, the rate of robberies has increased 255%, forcible rape 143%, aggravated assault 153% and murder 106%."[1]

Statistics are cold until they happen to you. I was told that at a fine private university in a small town in the West the girls don't go out of their rooms at night for fear of mugging or rape. The father who told me this said he had sent his daughter there to get her away from the dangerous areas of the large cities. This was worse.

There is no longer a safety zone in any city. A woman may be pistol-whipped while parking her car in an underground structure, or a man beaten on his way out of his office. Criminals have no respect for age, with older citizens living in many areas in a nightmare of fear. In New York City, police charged a gang of six teen-agers—one of whom was thirteen—with murdering three elderly and penniless men by asphyxiation. One man died with his prayer shawl stuffed into his mouth.

Man is a contradiction. On one side is hatred, depravity, and sin; on the other side is kindness, compassion, and love. Man is a helpless sinner on one hand and has capacities which would relate him to God on the other. No wonder Paul spoke of man's disease as "the mystery of iniquity."

Some people don't like the word *sin*. They believe this is for the other person, not them. But everyone recognises that the human race is sick and that whatever the disease is, it has affected all of life.

What is this thing called sin? The Westminster Confession defines it as "any want of conformity to or transgression of the law of God." Sin is anything contrary to the will of God.

THE BEGINNING OF SINNING

Where did sin begin and why did God allow it? The Bible hints at the answer to this riddle when it teaches that sin did not originate with man, but with the angel whom we know as Satan.

This was no ordinary angel, but the most magnificent of creatures!

The prophet Ezekiel describes this noble being this way: " 'You were the anointed cherub who covers; and I placed you there. You were on the holy mountain of God. ... You were blameless in your ways from the day you were created, *until unrighteousness was found in you*' " (Ezek. 28:14,15, emphasis mine). Here is a glimpse of where it started. In some unknown past, sin was found in the heart of this magnificent creature of heaven.

The prophet Isaiah gives us another hint of the origin of evil: " 'How you have fallen from heaven, O star of the morning [Lucifer], son of the dawn! You have been cut down to the earth, you who have weakened the nations! But you said in your heart, "*I will* ascend to heaven; *I will* raise my throne above the stars of God, and *I will* sit on the mount of assembly in the recesses of the north. *I will* ascend above the heights of the clouds; *I will* make myself like the Most High." Nevertheless you will be thrust down to Sheol, to the recesses of the pit' " (Isa. 14:12–15, emphasis mine).

There's the picture. Lucifer's sin was that of the five "I wills." He fell and became Satan because of his undue ambition. He wanted to be like God! He wanted to be equal to God. This was conceit in its strongest form. The New Testament gives us a glimpse of the sin of pride or conceit when it speaks of a person who might "become conceited and fall into the condemnation incurred by the devil" (1 Tim. 3:6).

FROM SATAN TO SINNERS

Sin began with the revolt of Lucifer and continued with man's revolt against God. In place of "living for God," sin substitutes "living for self."

The Bible makes it quite clear how sin entered the human race. In that luscious Garden of Eden there were many trees. One tree symbolised the knowledge of good and evil, and God in His wisdom said, "You shall not eat." Adam and Eve with one or two bites violated what they knew to be God's will (see Rom. 5:12–19; Gen. 3:1–8; 1 Tim. 2:13,14).

God could have created us as human robots who would respond mechanically to His direction. Obviously this would be a response over which man had no control. But instead, God created us in His image, and He desires that the creature worship the Creator as a response of love. This can be accomplished when "free will" is exercised. Love and obedience which are compelled do not satisfy. God wanted sons, not machines.

A pastor friend who was having dinner with us one evening told us about his son who was attending a state university and becoming "very wise." "Dad," he said to his father one day, "I'm not sure that when I get out of school I will be able to follow you in your simple Christian faith." Our friend looked his son in the eyes and replied, "Son, that is your freedom—your terrible freedom."

And that is what God gave Adam and Eve—and what He gives us—our freedom to choose. Our "terrible freedom." God gave humankind the gift of freedom. Our first parents had the choice: whether to love God or rebel and build their world without Him. The tree of the knowledge of good and evil was their test—and they flunked.

Sin is Rebellion

Why did Adam and Eve, with all Paradise to enjoy, choose to rebel? This cause of rebellion was "the lust of the flesh and the lust of the eyes and the boastful pride of life" (1 John 2:16). And this is the type of lust to which Eve submitted. "When the woman saw that the tree was good for food, and that it was a delight to the eyes, and that the tree was desirable to make one wise, she took from its fruit and ate; and she gave also to her husband with her, and he ate" (Gen. 3:6).

Centuries later, Christ faced the same three temptations in the wilderness. He overcame all of them and thereby showed us that it is possible to resist the temptations of Satan (Matt. 4:1—11).

The Ten Commandments tell us not to covet or lust. However, all moral law is more than a test; it's for our own good. Every law which God has given has been for our benefit. If a person breaks it, he is not only rebelling against God, he is hurting himself. God gave "the law" because he loves man. It is for man's benefit. God's commandments were given to protect and promote man's happiness, not to restrict it. God wants the best for man. To ask God to revise His commandments would be to ask Him to stop loving man.

Children usually accuse their parents of "not understanding" and being too strict. When a father says to his teen-ager, "Be in at 11 o'clock, and let me know exactly where you are going to be," he is protecting his child, not punishing him. God is a loving father.

When Adam and Eve broke God's commandment, they died spiritually and faced eternal death. The consequences of that act were immediate and fearful. Sin became and is the stubborn fact of life.

In our universe we live under God's law. In the physical realm, the planets move in split-second precision. There is no guesswork in the galaxies. We see in nature that everything is part of a plan which is harmonious, orderly, and obedient. Could a God who made the physical universe be any less exacting in the higher spiritual and moral order? God loves us with an infinite love, but He cannot and will not approve of disorder. Consequently, He has laid down spiritual laws which, if obeyed, bring harmony and fulfilment, but, if disobeyed, bring discord and disorder.

What were the results of Adam and Eve's sin? When both Satan and Adam challenged God's law, they did not break it; they broke themselves upon it. The life of beauty, freedom, and fellowship that Adam had known was gone; his sin resulted in a living death. Nature became cursed and the poison of sin infected the entire human family. The whole of creation was thrown into disharmony and the earth was now a planet in rebellion!

MISSING THE TARGET

One of the translations of the term *sin* in the New Testament means "a missing of the target." Sin is failure to live up to God's standards. All of us miss the target; there is not one person who is capable of fulfilling all of God's laws at all times.

For some people, even the standards of the world seem unattainable. One of the most intense and exciting spectacles we ever view is the World Olympics. Athletes who have trained for years, disciplining their minds and bodies to attain greater and greater goals, often fall short of their target. One of the finest figure skaters said she was particularly afraid that a fall would ruin her performance. She said, "Think how much time I've put into this, and how much other people have to help me. With one mistake, it could all go down the drain."[2]

In our spiritual lives we are constantly falling. There is no way we can turn in a perfect performance. King David said, "They have all turned aside; together they have become corrupt; there is no one who does good, not even one" (Ps. 14:3).

The prophet Isaiah confessed, "All of us like sheep have gone astray, each of us has turned to his own way" (Isa. 53:6).

We have all been touched by the sin of Adam. David said, "Behold, I was brought forth in iniquity, and in sin my mother conceived me" (Ps. 51:5). This doesn't mean that he was born out of wedlock, but that he inherited the tendency to sin from his parents.

"Why do we have to be punished for what Adam did?" Think about it. Would you have done any better than Adam? I know I wouldn't have.

We are all sinners by choice. When we reach the age of accountability and face the choice between good and evil, we will slip. We may choose to get angry, to lie, or to act selfishly. We will gossip or slander someone's character. None of us can really trust his heart, any more than we can trust a lion. In an animal preserve in East Africa the lions are allowed to roam around as if they were in their native habitat. People drive their cars or jeeps through the area, watching the lions, but are warned not to get near them. One woman rolled down the window in her car to get a better look, and without warning a lion charged, critically mauling her. That lion looked so tame, acted so docile, and yet became ferocious in one frightening instant.

The Bible applies this principle like this: "Sin is crouching at the door" (Gen. 4:7). Most of us are capable of almost anything, given the right circumstances. David was a classic example. Under circumstances of fleshly desire he took a woman who belonged to another man, then saw to it that her husband was murdered by putting him in the front line of battle.

You may be saying, "You make everyone out to be so rotten, and that isn't really true." Of course it isn't. A person may be a very moral individual and yet lack the love for God which is the fundamental requirement of the law.

Because we fail to meet God's requirements, we are guilty and under condemnation. Being guilty means that we deserve punishment. The very holiness of God reacts against sin: "For the wrath of God is revealed from heaven against all ungodliness and unrighteousness of men ... " (Rom. 1:18).

GUILTY OF WHAT?

The Bible says that sin is falling short of the glory of God. Many people are unaware of the nature of the target, so they can't understand why they are told that they are missing it. Let's imagine that someone puts a blindfold around your eyes and ties it so tight you are completely in the dark. Then you are told there is a dart board across the room and you are to hit it with a dart. You throw in exactly the direction you are told, but when the blindfold is removed you find that your dart is stuck in a lampshade, three feet from the target. You aimed in the right direction, but you missed.

This is where the world is today, missing the target. It's what Solomon meant when he said, "There is a way which seems right to a man, but its end is the way of death" (Prov. 14:12).

When God begins to open our blindfolds so that a small amount of light begins to seep through, we may begin to see an outline, at least, of the target. We can see, for instance, how God was beginning to reveal a general sense of direction to a girl who wrote me: "I'm not in any serious trouble or anything, but I do need the help of Jesus Christ. This is my first attempt to reach out to Him. I'm seventeen, and seriously want to consider myself a Christian. I'm reaching out ... please don't disappoint me."

Her letter shows that she senses "something" is wrong with her present life. Just what is wrong in her life and right in Christ's life she isn't yet able to say, but her life without Christ carries a kind of odour of death to it, and she wants to replace it by the fragrance of Christ. When she says she isn't in any "serious trouble," she means that she hasn't been arrested, or shamed before the community. But she has an uneasiness in her heart.

To help us see that something is terribly wrong in our lives and that death—spiritual death—will result, God gives us "the law," that is, a set of standards to sharpen our moral judgment so that we can recognise sin. The Ten Commandments form the backbone of the law. They are a giant x-ray machine to reveal the bone structure of our sinfulness. The first four x-ray plates concern our direct relation to God. The last six concern our relationships with others.

READING THE X-RAYS

"*You shall have no other gods before Me*" (Exod. 20:3). Another god is not necessarily a brass Buddha or a carved totem pole. Whatever captures our highest interest is our god. Sports can be a god—or work, or money. Sex may be a god to some, while travel may be a god to another. But our highest interest should be God. He alone is worthy of our worship. Jesus said that the great commandment was to love God with all our heart, soul, mind, and strength. If we were able to do this, we would be demonstrating that we have no other god except the Lord.

"*You shall not make for yourself an idol*" (Exod. 20:4). The first commandment dealt with whom we worship. This one concerns how. We are told to worship sincerely, with a heart for God. "Man looks at the outward appearance, but the Lord looks at the heart" (1 Sam. 16:7). When we sit in a church, full of piety, but ignoring God, we make an idol of the church building.

"*You shall not take the name of the Lord your God in vain*" (Exod. 20:7). This does not just apply to swearing, but even using the name for deity, such as God or Lord, without thinking of God Himself. If we vaguely mouth the words of a hymn, or call ourselves Christians without knowing Christ personally, we take the name of God in vain.

There is a story that Alexander the Great met a disreputable character whose name was also Alexander. Alexander the Great said, "Either change your way of life or change your name."

"*Remember the sabbath day, to keep it holy*" (Exod. 20:8). A day in seven set apart for special worship and rest is called for in Scripture. Jesus said, "The Sabbath was made for man, and not man for the Sabbath" (Mark 2:27). This means that we need that special day. God in His wisdom tells us that our bodies need it for rest, just as our spirits need it for worship. The practice of turning weekends into long periods of leisure and entertainment to the exclusion of worship means that we lose the advantage of both leisure and worship.

We know that a nation or an individual that works seven days a week suffers physically, psychologically, and spiritually. All machinery needs occasional rest.

"*Honour your father and your mother*" (Exod. 20:12). This passage sets no age limit on such honour. In addition, it does not say they must be honourable to be honoured. This doesn't necessarily mean that we must "obey" parents who may be dishonourable. Not only while we are children, but as long as our parents live, we must honour them if we are to obey God. Honour has many shapes: affection, humour, financial aid, respect. And yet, harsh words are often heard in the home more than anywhere else. We say things to our parents that we would never say to our friends at work or in church.

"*You shall not murder*" (Exod. 20:13). In the older translation of this command the word *kill* was used, but the original Hebrew properly refers to murder. The outward act of murder is the final act of many emotions. Behind it are the attitudes of irritation, envy, and hatred. Jesus said, "You have heard that men were told in the past, 'Do not murder; anyone who commits murder will be brought before the judge.' But now I tell you: whoever is angry with his brother will be brought before the judge; whoever calls his brother 'You good-for-nothing!' will be brought before the Council; and whoever calls his brother a worthless fool will be in danger of going to the fire of hell" (Matt. 5:21–22, TEV).

Is anyone able to say that he has never been angry with someone else? We all stand condemned before such a law, even if we have never forcefully taken someone's life.

"*You shall not commit adultery*" (Exod. 20:14). One scholar said: "One of the extraordinary things is that in the non-Christian religions time and time again immorality and obscenity flourish under the very protection of religion. It has often been said and said truly that chastity was the one completely new virtue which Christianity brought into this world."[3] Although that may be true, this commandment goes beyond chastity. It involves more than dishonouring a wife or husband by having sexual relations with others; it deals with the mentality which is occupied with sex. It means even looking at a man or woman with an attitude of desire or lust. To God, purity is first a matter of the heart, then of action.

Put in those terms you might say, "That's ridiculous. No one can live up to that commandment." And you would be right.

"*You shall not bear false witness against your neighbour*"

(Exod. 20:16). We think of a witness as one being in court. If on the stand we were to lie and say, "But, your honour, my dog was provoked into biting my neighbour. He started to hit my animal with a large stick and so he attacked in self-defence," when, in fact, your dog had taken a chunk out of your neighbour's leg without provocation, then you would be bearing a false witness.

But what if you gossip in a "harmless" way? The commandment is just as shattered!

"*You shall not covet*" (Exod. 20:17). When we take something that belongs to another, that's stealing. It is an act. Coveting is an attitude. When we desire something which belongs to someone else, that's coveting. How many marriages have ended in divorce because a man replaced thoughts about his own wife with thoughts about the desirability of his neighbour's wife? We are told not to covet anything, and that means our neighbour's new house, his car, his TV set, or the camper in his driveway.

RESULTS OF THE X-RAYS

Can anyone read the Ten Commandments with insight and not feel condemned by them? They reveal our hearts. The Apostle James made the comment that even one commandment broken would be enough to destroy us. If we are suspended over a pit by a chain of ten links, how many links have to break for us to fall into the pit? "For whoever keeps the whole law and yet stumbles in one point, he has become guilty of all" (James 2:10).

The Bible and our consciences tell us that we have seriously missed the target and are sinners. What does a holy God do? How does God deal with our sin?

We see a glimpse of this in the words of a young man who became painfully aware of the commandment, "You shall not steal." He said, "My life was not a rosy one. Before I was thirteen years old I was a thief in heart, word, and action. I had been arrested many times. I spent time in a boy's reformatory and less than a week after I left I was stealing again." He said that his family gave up on him and thought that his future was destroyed. One night he heard the gospel on television, found a Bible, and started to read it. As a result he asked Christ to forgive him for his past. He is now looking to Christ to build a new foundation and give him a new future.

How can God forgive us? What happens if sin becomes a pattern in our lives? What if we are really caught up in the sin syndrome? Is there any hope?

If there weren't any hope I wouldn't be writing this book! If there weren't answers, you probably wouldn't be reading!

6

Does God Have a Cure for Spiritual Disease?

A Doctor in Australia told me of a conversation between a man and his barber. As the scissors worked, the barber said, "Hmm—see you have a sore on your lip."

"Yep," said the man. "My cigarettes have done that."

"Well," said the barber, "it doesn't seem to be healing."

"Oh, it will—it will," replied the man confidently.

A month later he came into the shop again. His lip was split and ugly.

"Don't worry about it," he told the barber, "I've switched to a cigarette holder. It'll heal soon."

The barber had been concerned about his customer so he obtained some medical photographs that showed what lip cancer looked like. He urged his friend to compare them in the mirror with his own lip.

"Well, they look a lot alike," admitted the man, "but I'm not worried."

On the third month the man failed to come for his regular

haircut. When the barber called his friend's home to inquire about him he was told, "Oh, didn't you know? He died of cancer two days ago."

Sin is like cancer. It destroys step by step. Slowly, without our realising its insidious onslaught, it progresses until finally the diagnosis is pronounced: sick to death.

A man was describing to us how he had been brought up in a godly European home, had come to this country as a young man to seek his fortune, had been converted to Christ, and then had been sidetracked. Temptation yielded to another temptation until finally he found himself in what he thought was a hopeless condition. I'll never forget how he described the process. "It was like being in the ocean when there is a strong undertow," he said. "You don't realise how far you're drifting from shore until all of a sudden you find yourself beyond your depth, trying desperately to swim, but unable to hold your own against the outgoing tide."

But, unless we know some of the signs of danger, how can we seek help? We can find the help the Bible provides when we know the parts of a person that sin strikes and corrupts.

MIND ATTACK

A person may be brilliant in some areas, but inadequate about spiritual realities. The Bible teaches us that a veil lies over our minds and that before we can know Christ this veil must be lifted. Without this spiritual sight we cannot come to God.

You may have heard someone ask, "How can any intelligent person believe in the Bible and all those myths and contradictions?" (implying that the gospel of Jesus Christ is anti-intellectual). The implication is contrary to truth. Understanding demands the use of the mind, but when the mind is diseased by sin it is clouded and confused.

Joel Quinones was a living example of a person whose mind was under attack. I met him in San Diego and heard his amazing story.

Joel was first thrown into prison at the age of eight for trying to kill a sadistic man who had beaten him and burned him with cigarettes. When Joel was released, he came out a bundle of hatred and from then on did everything he could to show his scorn to society. As a result Joel found himself in San Quentin at the age of nineteen and spent the next eleven years there. He was turned over to the prison psychiatrists, who examined him, gave him shock treatments, and finally diagnosed him as "criminally insane."

Joel was placed in with incorrigibles. When they were fed. the food was placed on what appeared to be a large shovel with the handle long enough to push it under two separate security doors. "You don't even feed a tiger that way." Joel told us. "but that's the way they fed us."

After all those years in San Quentin. it was decided to get rid of the undesirable aliens, and Joel, along with a number of other Mexicans. was taken across the border and turned loose. He had a godly mother, a cook at a Bible school, who had been in the courtroom when Joel had been convicted for the first time. She had said to him then. "Joel, this isn't the end. Jesus has work for you to do."

When he was released in Mexico, his mother was there to greet him. Putting her arms around him. she said. "Joel, you need the Lord Jesus; you need to ask Him to forgive your sins, to give you a new heart and a new life."

Joel struggled with this. but before the Lord was finished with him he was a transformed person. He went to Bible school, married one of the graduates. and is today a prison chaplain in Mexico. He has won so many prisoners to Christ that he is busy trying to build a halfway house, a "City of Refuge" to which these prisoners can come for rehabilitation before returning to normal life.

Sin had affected Joel's mind. but the transforming power of Christ had given him new gifts.

As I write this, I'm looking at a bone-handled knife with a five-inch blade that once belonged to Joe Medina. Joe's story is one of the most unbelievable, comic, awe-inspiring demonstrations of the power of God in what the ordinary person would have termed a hopeless life that I have ever heard. Mind attack? Joe simply couldn't think straight.

Joe was brought up in a Bronx ghetto. His mother and both of his grandmothers were spirit mediums. The streets of New York had been his home since babyhood, and gang warfare, knife fighting, stealing, and lying were simply a way of life. He was one of those disenchanted, rebellious youths of the sixties—a drug-user and accomplished thief.

Joe, however, went to a meeting at which Akbar Haqq, one of our associate evangelists, was speaking. Before the evening was over, Joe had given his heart to Jesus Christ. The day after his conversion, one of his best buddies was trying to induce Joe to go with him to get drugs and Joe didn't want to be bothered. The friend pulled a knife and threatened to cut Joe up. That was a big mistake. Joe was small, but like lightning with a knife, and before he knew what had happened, he had plunged the knife (yes, the one on my desk) into his buddy. The boy he attacked was in the hospital for two weeks.

Joe had no Christian background to fall back on and he had many ups and downs in his spiritual life. He enrolled in a small college near us but quit school before the year was up. I'm still not sure what his reason was, but I think he had some vague notion that he had to get back to share his faith with his buddies in the Bronx.

My wife talked to Joe before he left and urged him to come to Madison Square Garden, where we were having a meeting. I found out later that Joe had rounded up some of his tough buddies and gotten to the Garden at 7:30, only to find it closed because it was full, and the policeman wouldn't let him in. There had been a threat on my life that night and the policemen were taking a dim view of any suspicious-looking characters. Joe and his friends qualified for that description.

They went into a huddle and decided to rush the police. They succeeded in getting to the top floor of the Garden but suddenly found themselves face to face with a wall of plainclothes men advancing on them. Turning to run the other way, they confronted another formidable wall of police. They were thrown out of the Garden without further ceremony. When I heard about this later I thought, "Oh no! Just the ones we were trying to reach!"

However, Joe was undaunted and brought his sister and brother the next night. They both came forward to receive Christ.

Joe had a lot of trouble for a while getting values straightened out. He called Ruth one time and said he had to see her. When he arrived, she could tell something was wrong. "What have you done now, Joe?" she asked.

"Ruth, I robbed a filling station."

"Oh, Joe, why did you do that?"

"Well, it's this way—I have this buddy, you know. Well, he needed some money and he'd never robbed a filling station before. Golly, Ruth, I felt it was my Christian duty to help him."

Ruth asked him how much he had taken and then asked him if his buddy were a Christian. He was not, Joe said. Ruth explained to Joe that he would have to be responsible for returning the entire amount. Joe looked as if she had hit him in the stomach with her fist. She then asked him point-blank if he had anything else in his possession that he had stolen. He looked at her in amazement and exclaimed, as if that were the dumbest question ever asked, "Everything I own!"

Joe returned all the stolen goods. After more advances and retreats in his Christian growth than I care to relate, he was finally admitted to Columbia Bible College. In his senior year he became vice president of the student body and is today a graduate student there with an amazing knowledge and love of the Bible.

On a recent weekend he came to visit us and the Presbyterian pastor of our community, Calvin Thielman, asked him to give his testimony and talk about his ministry. Joe told how he related to drug-users, the dropouts, the rebels. His story was full of such wit, humour, and compassion that the audience was left with the reassurance that "nobody's hopeless."

Only those who knew Joe from the beginning can fully appreciate the marvels of the new birth in this young man's life. His mind had been so attacked by sin that it took a long time for the healing process. We are born again as babies, not mature Christians, and babies need a lot of love and patience!

The Bible teaches that sin affects the mind, whether that mind is of superior intelligence or average. A person may be intellectually brilliant, but spiritually ignorant. "A natural man does not accept the things of the Spirit of God; ... and he cannot understand them, because they are spiritually appraised" (1 Cor 2:14).

An intellectual mind can be turned into a first-class mind when Christ penetrates the heart. Gerhard Dirks, one of the most brilliant men in the world, is reported to have an IQ of 208. He has over 140 patents with IBM and has even attempted theoretically to reconstruct the human brain. He became completely bewildered and shaken, however, when confronted with the complexity and utter impossibility of such a reconstruction. He didn't know what to do or where to run. His choice was twofold: either the human brain came about by a fantastic chance or by intelligent planning. When faced with the alternative he knew he had only one choice, and he became a believer in God as it was revealed to him through Jesus Christ, whose intellect he could not surpass.

Dr. Boris Botsenko, a brilliant Russian physicist-mathematician, was attending a conference of scientists in Edmonton, and in his hotel picked up a Gideon Bible. He read it and through it accepted Jesus Christ and was born again. He is now in the research department of the University of Toronto.

ATTACK ON THE WILL

Sin attacks another facet of our being—the will. Jesus said, "Every one who commits sin is the slave of sin" (John 8:34). Even in countries where there is political freedom, there are millions who live under the tyranny of pride, jealousy, or prejudice. Countless others are slaves to alcohol, barbiturates or narcotics. They possess traits or are consumed by desires they hate but are powerless in their grip. They want to be free, and some search for freedom through avenues offered by other men. But Christ said, "You shall know the truth, and the truth shall make you free" (John 8:32). Christ is the truth.

I have known many persons who found freedom from the bondage of will and desire. On May 9, 1972, in a little church outside Nashville, Tennessee, a pastor gave a gospel invitation and a man named Johnny Cash got up and went down the aisle and knelt at the altar of the church. Johnny Cash says that he gave his life to Jesus Christ that day. Here is a man whose life has been hurt by drugs and imprisonment, and who has become a hero to the world of country music. He is now a force for good in the world and is being used in the cause of Christ.

I have in my possession a hashish pipe as a reminder of a young man who was a slave to drugs. He had made a terrible mess of his life and also the life of the girl he loved. As a result, he drove to a lonely, deserted parkway where he slit his wrists. Evidently he didn't do a very good job, because the blood wasn't coming out fast enough and he thought at that rate it was going to take him too long to die. So he crawled under the tailpipe of his car with the motor still going, covered himself with a blanket, and proceeded to inhale the fumes.

He said that while he became drowsy from the fumes he uttered a prayer asking God to forgive him for what he was doing. Suddenly a horrible black feeling came over him and he knew that what he was about to do did not please God. In his weakness, with bleeding wrists and drugged mind, he drove to a pastor's home. The pastor took him to the hospital. After the young man was treated, the pastor explained to him that Christ alone can make atonement for our sins and give us release from guilt and the joy of being forgiven.

This young man is now happily married and is a positive influence on the lives of others.

Unresolved hatred is a tyranny which can make anyone a slave to sin as it attacks the will. Just a few years ago Dr. William P. Wilson, Professor of Psychiatry at Duke University Medical Centre, systematically took Bibles away from his patients at the centre. But his life and medical practice have been transformed by the power of Jesus Christ, and he now uses the insights he has gained from the gospel in treating his patients. He keeps copies of the Bible in his office and gives them out. Dr. Wilson says, "One of the greatest causes of mental illness is unresolved guilt. Feelings of shame, inadequacy, missing the mark, not measuring up, are some sources of guilt feelings. The answer to guilt is grace and the new birth. The new birth leads to the forgiveness of sin."

Forgiveness is hard for many to believe. Dr. Warren Wiersbe of Chicago calls forgiveness "the greatest miracle in the Bible."

I have a letter from a young man who said, "In 1971 I was a drug-dealing dropout from Northwestern University. During your Chicago Crusade I came forward at the invitation and prayed for the Lord to save me, even though I personally didn't feel bad about my ungodly practices. I also asked that He forgive me my sins (I could intellectually conceive of them, but not personally feel them) and that He would make Himself known in a personal way.

"I was expecting a lightning bolt from heaven to knock me down, or for God to put me through a mental breakdown so He could straighten out my mind and use it for His glory. Needless to say, He didn't do that. I began to feel quite disappointed and also somewhat scared and thought this God thing might easily turn out to be a hoax after all. At that instant a middle-aged, short-haired, suit-wearing, Bible-carrying counsellor came up to me and put a Jesus sticker on my shirt and shook my hand. 'God bless you, young man,' he said. Think of it! This establishment dude shaking my hand—me, a freaked-out hippie. The love of God coming through him showed me that Jesus loved me regardless of how I dressed or abused society. That simple act hit me and I suddenly realised the simplicity of God's salvation. He didn't want to put me through pain of a mental breakdown—all He wanted me to do was to receive His Son as I had just done!"

WHEN CONSCIENCE FAILS

Sin not only affects the mind and the will, but also the conscience. A person becomes very slow to detect the approach of sin. It's like telling an untruth: the first time you tell a story it really bothers you; but with repetition your conscience is no longer your guide, and soon the lie is woven so strong that you are convinced it's the truth. You no longer have sensitivity to things you know are wrong.

One day Joe Medina, to whom I referred earlier in the chapter, called Ruth from a telephone booth and said, "Ruth, I'm not drunk, but I just wanted to tell you something."

Ruth asked him what he was doing in a phone booth. He explained that he was riding around with a buddy who had a fifth of whisky with him. Joe explained that his friend didn't have a North Carolina driver's licence and shouldn't drive the car, especially while drinking. So Joe said, with his typical logic, "Ruth, I felt it was my Christian duty to drink that fifth of whisky for him."

The patience of my wife never ceases to amaze me. She said, "Joe, you drank that fifth of whisky because you wanted to drink that fifth of whisky."

There was a long pause. Then, "Ruth, you're exactly right."

Joe had been trained in calling badness "good." He knew how to lie, cheat, and rationalise out of any situation. But for the grace of God, he would still be that way today.

The results of the infection of no longer knowing the difference between good and evil are reflected in every part of the Scriptures. When David first looked at Bathsheba, a train of events began which led from his adultery to deceit to murder. David was forgiven for his sins, but he had to pay the natural consequences. He reaped a bitter harvest and his reign was clouded with constant trouble.

In view of the way we allow our consciences to become dulled, it is amazing that God is so patient. The Bible says, "The Lord is not slack concerning His promise, as some men count slackness, but is longsuffering toward us, not willing that any should perish, but that all should come to repentance" (2 Pet. 3:9, AV).

No matter how patient God is, He is also just. When man hardens his heart, God continues to speak. But man cannot hear. Genesis 6:3 says, "My spirit shall not always strive with man." Eventually, if God sees that man won't repent, "There is a sin unto death" (1 John 5:16, AV). This refers to blasphemy against the Holy Spirit, which is final rejection of God's plan of salvation, and it is also described in Hebrews 6:4–6:

"For in the case of those who have once been enlightened and have tasted of the heavenly gift and have been made partakers of the Holy Spirit, and have tasted the good word of God and the powers of the age to come, and then have fallen away, it is impossible to renew them again to repentance, since they again crucify to themselves the Son of God, and put Him to open shame."

When a man's conscience is gone he uses all kinds of excuses to justify his action. He blames his family, his business associates, his bad breaks, anything. He can cheat on his income tax because the laws are unjust. He can cheat on his wife (or a wife can be unfaithful to her husband) because the other one is cold—or thoughtless. The good and bad are gone and life is lived in grey tones.

In Athens the columns and statues of the Parthenon have been eroding in recent years at an accelerated rate. It hasn't been storms or time which have caused the imminent destruction of these priceless ancient works of art, but the pollution of the wastes of modern society. In the same way, it's not the heavy storms of life that erode us, but the insidious, gradual pollution of sin which leads to our destruction.

SICK TO DEATH

Crime requires punishment and sin has a penalty. Although this may be a subject we would like to ignore, it is an unavoidable fact. Not only does everyone suffer as a result of sin in this life, but everyone must face the judgment to come. "For the wages of sin is death" (Rom. 6:23).

First, there is *physical death*. The Bible says, "It is appointed for men to die once" (Heb. 9:27). Incidentally, this completely rules out the possibility of reincarnation.

Death is inevitable and unpredictable in many cases. For each of us there is a day, an hour, a minute, when physically we are no longer earth beings. If God had not given the judgment of physical death, the earth would soon become uninhabitable, because men would live forever in their sins.

Because life is brief, the Bible teaches that we must "Prepare to meet [our] God" (Amos 4:12). In the course of my life I have known many people who are thoroughly prepared to meet God. There is a startling difference between them and people who have lived a life without God.

I will never forget the summer of 1973. That was the year that one of the greatest Christians I ever knew entered heaven. He was my father-in-law, Dr. L. Nelson Bell. Dr. Bell served Christ for years in China as a missionary surgeon. In 1972 he had been Moderator of the Presbyterian Church in the United States, the highest honour his denomination could bestow. The night before he died he spoke for the World Missions Conference in a large auditorium in Montreat.

At the end of his talk he said, "Before I pray I have a few

words to say. After hearing that singing, no one can deny that our Presbyterian Church is waking up. Now in this place there are two groups of people. There are those who know they are saved and love the Lord Jesus Christ, and there are those here who as yet may not know Christ. My hope is that before you leave this place you will come to know him as your personal Lord and Saviour. The Lord said, 'Behold, I stand at the door and knock; if any man hear my voice, and open the door, I will come in to him, and will sup with him and he with me.' "

Those were the last words that Dr. Bell said in public. That night he went to sleep and when he awoke he was in the presence of his Lord. His life had come full circle. His favourite hymn was "All the Way My Saviour Leads Me," and when I saw him that morning, it was a great comfort to see the face of one so peaceful.

He was prepared to meet God.

I remember hearing of the last words said by Pearl Goode, a wonderful woman who through the years was one of our most faithful prayer supporters, often going into seclusion and praying night and day for the Crusade team wherever they were. She walked in such close fellowship with God that when it was her time to go, she sat up in bed and said, "Well, there He is. There's Jesus!" She was prepared to meet God.

In the summer of 1976 there was a flash flood in Colorado that took the lives of a great many people. Among the victims were some young Christian girls who had been at a retreat in the mountains. The men who had the job of searching out the bodies of those who were killed reported later that most of the people had expressions of horror on their faces, but they were astounded to see that every one of the girls appeared to be at peace. They were prepared to meet their God.

Life is so short. The Bible says that we must be prepared to meet God at all times. We never know when we step into our car, walk out the door of our home, or just open our eyes to a new day, what lies ahead. " 'Since his days are determined, the number of his months is with Thee, and his limits Thou hast set so that he cannot pass' " (Job 14:5).

The second dimension of death is *spiritual death*. Millions of people on earth are walking around physically alive, but spiritually dead. When your eyes and ears become attuned to the cries of others, you hear those who say they are empty and lost. They are separated from the source of life and like a lamp which is unattached, they are dark and lifeless. The lamp may be very expensive, may have a beautiful shade which draws attention, but has no light without being plugged into the source of energy. Jesus said, "I am the life."

Newspapers and magazines throughout the world carried the story of the suicide of Freddie Prinze. At the age of twenty-two he had attained one of the highest status roles in show business. He was the darling of television and had just performed for an incoming president at the Inaugural gala in Washington. Yet something was terribly wrong in the life of this talented comedian. A close friend, comedian David Brenner, explained to *Time* magazine. "There was no transition in Freddie's life. It was an explosion. It's tough to walk off a subway at age 19 and then step out of a Rolls Royce the next day." Producer James Komack, also a close confidant, said, "Freddie saw nothing around that would satisfy him. He would ask me 'Is this what it is? Is this what it's all about?' " Mr. Komack said, "His real despondency, whether he could articulate it or not, concerned the questions: 'Where do I fit in? Where is my happiness?' I would tell him, 'God, Freddie, your happiness is right here. You're a star.' He'd say, 'No. That's not happiness for me any more.' " As *Time* magazine commented at the end of the story, "For one of the most singular escape stories in ghetto history, escape was not enough."[1]

We may be physically alive, but spiritually dead, like the woman who is described as "dead even while she lives" (1 Tim. 5:6).

The third dimension of death is *eternal death*. This may be a subject which most try to avoid. We hear a lot about "hell on earth," but there is another hell which is more real and certain, and that's the hell of eternal death. Jesus Himself spoke frequently about hell. He warned of a hell to come. The Scripture teaches us that we'll be in hell alone and bearing pain alone. There is no fellowship in hell except fellowship with darkness. I have heard some people say, "If I thought my father [or some other loved one] were in hell, that's where I would want to be, too!" What an illusion! Hell is the loneliest place imaginable.

Jesus warned men, "And these will go away into eternal punishment" (Matt. 25:46). He also said, "The Son of Man will send forth His angels and they will gather out of His kingdom all stumbling blocks, and those who commit lawlessness, and will cast them into the furnace of fire; in that place there shall be weeping and gnashing of teeth" (Matt. 13:41,42).

There is never such an urgency to talk about eternity as there is when physical death confronts us. A friend of mine told me that the day after her son was killed in an airplane accident, while their house was full of people offering love and consolation, something went wrong with the furnace. A repair man was called. After looking at the heater, he said, "Lady, if you had waited a little while longer to call me that furnace might have blown up." In the midst of her own grief she paused, looked the repair man squarely in the eyes. "There's only one thing that's important right now," she said. "If that furnace had exploded while you were working on it, do you know for sure where you would spend eternity?"

Before he left the house he learned how to have assurance of his eternal destiny.

TWO FACES OF MAN

Man has two faces. One shows his ingenuity, his capacity to create, to be kind, to honour truth. The other face reveals him using his ingenuity maliciously. We see him doing kind acts in a shrewd manner in order to forward a private desire. We see one side of him enjoying a sunset, but at the same time working in a job that fills the atmosphere with waste products that nearly obscure the sunset. His search for truth often degenerates into a rat race to discover a scientific fact so the credit will be his.

Man is both dignified and degraded.

The need for spiritual rebirth is evident to the most casual observer of human nature. Man is fallen and lost, alienated from God. From the very beginning, all attempts to recover man from his lostness have revealed one or the other of two ways.

PLAN A AND PLAN B

Remember Cain and Abel? The sons of Adam and Eve represent Plan A and Plan B of salvation. One of them, Cain, came his own way: he initiated Plan A; the other, Abel, was obedient and came God's way, Plan B.

Cain was the self-sufficient materialist and religious humanist. He brought to the altar an expression of his own labours; he became the prototype of all who dare approach God without the shedding of blood.

Cain's way didn't work for him. It has never worked for anyone, and it will not work today. Only God can properly diagnose our disease and provide the cure. God chose blood as the means of our redemption. The Apostle John wrote that Jesus Christ "washed us from our sins in his own blood" (Rev. 1:5, AV).

When Jesus Christ, the perfect God-man, shed His blood on the cross, He was surrendering His pure and spotless life to death as an eternal sacrifice for man's sin. Once and for all, God made complete provision for the cure of man's sins. Without the blood of Christ, it is a fatal disease.

Each of us makes his choice between the two ways—man's way or God's way. Which?

II

God's Answer

7

The Man Who Is God

IT'S JUST AFTER Christmas as I write this chapter. The cards are still coming in each day, bulging the mailbox and dazzling the eye. Many of them have pictures of Jesus, some as a baby in a rough-hewn cradle, others as a shepherd, surrounded by children. The world is fascinated with how He might look. From the magnificent cathedrals of Europe to Sunday school classrooms in the U.S.A., we see pictures of artists' conceptions of Jesus. I was in Africa a few days before Christmas and saw Jesus depicted as a black baby. Last year we were in the Orient just before Christmas and saw Him depicted as an Oriental.

What is the image the world has of Jesus Christ? Some visualise Him as a pale, blue-eyed man, smiling rather weakly beneath an ethereal halo. In America, the new popular Jesus is a handsome, virile type with robust charm and appeal. Probably Jesus looked Middle Eastern, with a swarthy-coloured skin—we really don't know. And it's just as well that we don't know what He really looked like physically—because today He belongs to the world!

No matter how we imagine Him to be, Jesus Christ has no
stronger portrait than the one in the Bible. It is a picture of the
Man who is God. The claim that Jesus Christ is deity is the focal
point for all belief. It is the foundation of Christianity. Since the
quickest way to destroy any edifice is to tear out or weaken its
base, men have always tried to disprove, ignore, or scoff at the
claims of Christ. However, our hope of redemption from sin is
dependent upon the deity of Christ.

Who is he?

JESUS: UNIQUE IN ALL WAYS

We know that Jesus lived. He was a man in history, as well as
a man for all times. Tacitus, perhaps the greatest Roman historian
born in the first century, speaks of Jesus. Josephus, a Jewish
historian born A.D. 37, tells of the crucifixion of Jesus. A
contemporary Bible scholar said that "the latest edition of the
Encyclopaedia Britannica uses 20,000 words in describing this
person, Jesus. His description took more space than was given to
Aristotle, Cicero, Alexander, Julius Caesar, Buddha, Confucius,
Mohammed or Napoleon Bonaparte."[1]

Rousseau said, "It would have been a greater miracle to invent
such a life as Christ's than to be it."

Jesus lived, taught, and died on earth in a small area of the
Middle East, mostly in what is in Israel today. That is a confirmed
fact of history.

HIS INTELLECT

Many men in history have been admired and many have been
given honours for their intellectual achievements, but no man has
had the incisive intellect of Jesus. In all circumstances, whether
tired from a long journey, or plagued by His enemies, Jesus was
able to confound some of the greatest minds of His day.

He had three years of intellectual encounters with the religious leaders of His day. These men often tried to put Him on the spot by asking questions which were difficult to answer. On one occasion, when He was teaching in the temple, the chief priests and elders questioned Him belligerently. They asked, "By what authority are You doing these things, and who gave You this authority?" (Matt. 21:23).

Here were the men who had control of all the religious teaching, and this Jesus, a carpenter from Nazareth, who was not their pupil, was teaching in their territory. Can you imagine what would happen at one of our prestigious seminaries if the janitor suddenly stepped onto the platform and began to instruct the students?

Jesus answered the question of the religious authorities with another question. "I will ask you one thing too, which if you tell Me, I will also tell you by what authority I do these things. The baptism of John was from what source, from heaven or from men?"

Now John the Baptist had not been ordained by them either, and he had urged his followers to obey Jesus. The religious leaders were thrown into confusion. They knew if they said "From heaven," that Jesus would say, "Then why didn't you believe him?" On the other hand, if they answered "From men," they feared that the people would become irate, because they believed John was a prophet. So they simply said, "We don't know."

Jesus replied, "Neither will I tell you by what authority I do these things" (Matt. 21:27).

Jesus possessed a mental agility that has astounded scholars for 2,000 years.

HIS FRANKNESS

No matter what the consequences, Jesus was very open and frank. The members of the religious establishment of His day were meticulously following certain rites for cleansing the dishes they ate from each day. Using this practice as an illustration, Jesus said, "Woe to you, scribes and Pharisees, hypocrites! For you clean the outside of the cup and of the dish, but inside they are full of robbery and self-indulgence. You blind Pharisee, first clean the inside of the cup and of the dish, so that the outside of it may become clean also" (Matt. 23:25, 26).

The charge Jesus made is just as applicable today. True belief in God is inward and has to do with a personal commitment and attitude, rather than strict observance of rituals and rules. Most of us would be reticent to speak so frankly to church leaders of our time. Jesus, however, was a man who was frank, bold and honest in every situation.

HIS OPENNESS

Jesus had the ability to understand all people, no matter what their position in society. On one occasion He was dining with a prominent religious leader named Simon. While they were eating, a repentant prostitute came into the hall where the meal was being served and began to wash the feet of Jesus with her tears and dry them with her hair. The religious leader was shocked and began to look at Jesus with doubt. He thought, "If this man were a prophet He would know who and what sort of person this woman is who is touching Him ... "

Jesus, sensing his thoughts, told him this story: "A certain money-lender had two debtors; one owed five hundred denarii [a denarius was then a day's wage], and the other fifty. When they were unable to repay, he graciously forgave them both. Which of them therefore will love him more?"

Simon must have wondered, what's the purpose of this story? He probably shrugged as he answered, "I suppose the one to whom he forgave more."

Jesus told him that was the right answer. Then He reminded Simon that when He had come into his house as a guest, Simon had ignored all the normal courtesies of the day. "You gave Me no water for My feet, but she has wet My feet with tears, and wiped them with her hair. You gave Me no kiss; but she, since the time I came in, has not ceased to kiss My feet."

Then Jesus turned to the woman and reassured her that her sins had been forgiven.

The other guests at the dinner party were astounded. They asked, "Who is this man who even forgives sins?" (Luke 7).

We know that Jesus often dined with the social elite but defended the social outcasts.

HIS FORGIVING SPIRIT

His opponents were powerful and persistent. They mocked Him, plotted against Him, and finally manoeuvred the crowds to support His death by crucifixion.

As He was hanging on the cross, bleeding and suffering from the pain and the hot sun, many jeered at Him, saying, "Save Yourself, and come down from the cross!" (Mark 15:30).

Under such extreme circumstances, Jesus exhibited a trait that was beyond our comprehension. He spoke to God the Father and said, "Father forgive them; for they do not know what they are doing" (Luke 23:34).

How many mere men could forgive their persecutors under such brutal circumstances?

HIS MORAL AUTHORITY

The pictures of Jesus as a vague, colourless man do not fit the true account of His strength and moral authority. At the end of His life the establishment, both religious and political, had united together to end His work by sending officers to arrest Him. The burly henchmen approached Jesus, but stopped to listen to what He was saying. They returned to their superiors without Him.

"Why didn't you bring Him?" they were asked.

The officers replied in astonishment, "Never did a man speak

the way this man speaks" (John 7:45, 46). They were
experiencing what the crowds of ordinary people already knew.
"The multitudes were amazed at His teaching," Matthew
reported, "for He was teaching them as one having authority, and
not as their scribes" (Matt. 7:28, 29).

Jesus Christ lived the type of life He taught. There are many
men we know who are noble, intelligent, frank, open, and who
speak with authority. But only in Jesus do we find the human
characteristics which we would expect God to display if He were
to become a man.

Jesus' claim to deity is fully supported by His character. He
was unique in history.

MORE THAN JUST A MAN

If this were all we had to say about Jesus Christ, He would
have very little more to offer than many great men of history.
However, the uniqueness of Christ is that in His life on earth He
displayed every known attribute or characteristic of deity.

What is an attribute? One Bible scholar offered this simple
definition: "The attributes of God are those distinguishing
characteristics of the nature of God which are inseparable from
the idea of deity, and which constitute the basis and grounds for
His various manifestations to His creatures."[2]

Jesus Christ was the supreme manifestation of God. "God was
in Christ reconciling the world to Himself" (2 Cor. 5:19).

He was no ordinary man. Several hundred years before He was
born, Isaiah, the prophet, said, "Behold, a virgin will be with
child and bear a son" (Isa. 7:14). No other man in all history
could say that his mother was a virgin. The Scriptures teach that
He did not have a human father; if He had, He would have
inherited the sins and infirmities that all men have, since "that
which is born of the flesh is flesh" (John 3:6). Since He was
conceived not by natural means, but by the Holy Spirit, He stands
as the one man who came forth pure from the hand of God. He

could stand before His fellowmen and ask, "Which of you can truthfully accuse Me of one single sin?" (John 8:46, *The Living Bible*). He was the only man since Adam who could say, 'I am pure."

If we honestly probe our minds, we have to admit that there are mysteries about the incarnation that none of us can ever understand. In fact, Paul speaks of God, manifest in the flesh, as a "mystery" (1 Tim. 3:16).

Paul explained the Man who is God in another epistle: "Have this attitude in youselves which was also in Christ Jesus, who, although He existed in the form of God, did not regard equality with God a thing to be grasped, but emptied Himself, taking the form of a bond-servant, and being made in the likeness of men" (Phil. 2:5–7).

First, *God is Holy*. This is a characteristic possessed by Jesus Christ which is central to the entire Christian faith. What does "holiness" mean? It is a term used in reference to people, places, and sometimes circumstances. However, this very common word, often misused and misunderstood, means "self-affirming purity." No mere human being now or ever could possess pure holiness and moral perfection.

In the Old Testament, God is described as "holy in all his works" (Ps. 145:17, AV) and the prophet Isaiah, in his vision of the Lord God, declares, "Holy, holy, holy, is the Lord of hosts" (Isa. 6:3). In the New Testament this unique attribute is possessed by Jesus Christ, the holy child, the sinless man. Thus Jesus Christ had a characteristic that only God could possess.

Second, *God is also just*. In order to guard His holiness, God must exercise justice. Since all sin is an offence to God, the principle of God's justice is vital to an orderly universe, just as a nation must have certain laws and codes. But unlike human government, which uses justice in ways that are suitable to the rulers or heads of government, God's justice is pure; no mistake is ever made.

Jesus Christ was just. During His earthly career He exhibited this characteristic when He drove the racketeers out of the temple with a whip. He is also described as faithful and just in forgiving us our sins. When He died for our sins it was "the Just" dying for the unjust.

Third, *God is mercy*. This characteristic of deity was seen in the entire life of Jesus Christ. When the woman who was an adulteress was brought before the authorities and condemned to be stoned, Jesus defended her with the charge, "Let him who is without sin cast the first stone." Her accusers retreated in embarrassment. Jesus Christ, exhibiting God's mercy, told her to go and sin no more. The love, mercy, and compassion of Jesus come out time after time throughout His public ministry. In the opening address that Jesus gave at His home town of Nazareth, He had quoted Isaiah the prophet, "The Spirit of the Lord is upon Me, because He anointed Me to preach the gospel to the poor. He has sent Me to proclaim release to the captives, and recovery of sight to the blind, to set free those who are downtrodden, to proclaim the favourable year of the Lord" (Luke 4:18).

Fourth, *God is love*. The first songs children learn in Sunday school, when they are barely able to carry a tune, are about God's love. A child can understand God's love, but the depths are so infinite that an adult finds it difficult to fathom. God's love is the continuing result of His holiness, justice, and mercy.

As a holy God, He hates sin and can have no fellowship with sin. Because the Bible tells us that the soul that sins must surely die, we can see that separation from God is a result of sin. However, because God is also mercy, He longs to save the guilty sinner and must then provide a substitute which will satisfy His divine justice. He provided that substitute in Jesus Christ. There is God's love: "For God so loved the world, that He gave His only begotten Son, that whoever believes in Him should not perish, but have eternal life" (John 3:16).

GOD AND JESUS CHRIST THE SAME

Fifth, Jesus Christ possesses the three great "omni's" of God. This prefix means "completely or all' and when used within the word *omnipotent* it means that the possessor has all power. The dictionary has one word to describe the Omnipotent, and that is God.

While a man on earth, Jesus Christ performed many miracles. He raised people from the dead; He took a few loaves and fishes and multiplied them to feed thousands; He cured the chronically sick and healed the crippled. But why should this be surprising? Jesus said, "All power is given unto me in heaven and in earth" (Matt. 28:18, AV). That is a startling statement if it were made by any ordinary man. Only God could make such a claim.

Jesus Christ was *omniscient*. This means that He knew all things, and He still knows all things. The Scriptures say, "Jesus knowing their thoughts" (Matt. 9:4); "He knew all men ... He Himself knew what was in man" (John 2:24, 25); "In whom are hidden all the treasures of wisdom and knowledge" (Col. 2:3).

Do you know anyone of your acquaintance, or any person in history, who knew everything? Have you ever heard of a person who could know, without a mistake, the minds of men? Only an all-powerful God knows everything, and Jesus Christ was omniscient.

Probably no idea is more difficult for man to comprehend than the thought of *omnipresence*. How can God be everywhere at once? From our viewpoint we are bound by time and space. We are physical creatures who can only be one place at a time. We frequently complain, "I can't be everywhere at once!" God transcends time and space, and so does Jesus Christ. He existed before time began. "Before Abraham was born, I AM" (John 8:58). "He is before all things" (Col. 1:17).

Jesus is not earthbound. He said, "Wherever two or more of you are gathered together in My Name there am I in the midst of you." He can be with a gathering of believers in a primitive hut in

New Guinea or a businessmen's luncheon in Dallas. He can be at the supper table of a family or in the banquet hall of royalty. Jesus Christ is omnipresent.

Jesus Christ claimed to be God. He said "I and the Father are one" (John 10:30) and, "He who beholds Me beholds the One who sent Me" (John 12:45). He made it very clear when He spoke to the religious leaders of His time about who He was. "I am He who bears witness of Myself, and the Father who sent Me bears witness of Me" (John 8:18). Members of the local church hierarchy said to Him, 'Where is Your Father?" Jesus answered, "You know neither Me, nor My Father; if you knew Me, you would know My Father also" (John 8:19).

Christ represents Himself as having been "sent from God" and being "not of this world." He declares that He is "the light of the world," "the way, the truth, and the life," and "the resurrection and the life." He promises eternal life to everyone who believes in Him as Lord and Saviour.

Knowing the claims of Jesus Christ, you are faced with this vital decision—

WHAT WILL YOU DO WITH JESUS?

Question: Who do you think Jesus Christ is? If He is not who He claimed to be, He is a deceiver or an egomaniac. We cannot settle for a middle-of-the-road answer that He was "a good man," or the modern form of adulation as a "superstar." He Himself eliminates a neutral answer. Either we decide He is a liar or a lunatic, or we must declare Him to be Lord.

In light of the evidence of Scripture and the physical fact of the Resurrection, the only wise conclusion is that He is God, worthy of our worship and trust. When I decide to be a Christian, I am deciding who Jesus Christ is. Trust in Him makes me a believer in Him and leads to being truly alive!

OUT OF HIS PRIVATE WILDERNESS

We heard about a young couple who were separated during World War II. While the father was gone the mother gave birth to a baby girl. The months passed and the mother kept a large picture of her husband on the desk so that the little girl would grow up knowing what her daddy looked like. She learned to say "Daddy" and associated the name with the picture on the desk. Finally the day came when her father returned home from the war. The whole family gathered to watch the little girl when she saw her father for the first time. Imagine their disappointment when she would have nothing whatever to do with him. Instead, she ran to the photograph on the desk, saying, "That's my daddy." Day after day the family had to blink back the tears as they saw the young father on his knees trying his best to get acquainted with his little daughter, explaining as simply as he could that he was her daddy. But each time she would shake her head, then run to the picture on the desk and exclaim, "That's my daddy." This went on for some time, but one day something happened. The little girl, having gone repeatedly to the picture on the desk, returned to her father and looked carefully into his face. Then she went back to the picture on the desk and studied it. The family held their breath. After several trips the little face lit up as the child exclaimed excitedly, "They're both the same daddy!"

C. S. Lewis described his experience: "You must picture me alone in that room in Magdalen, night after night, feeling, whenever my mind lifted even for a second from my work, the steady unrelented approach of Him whom I so earnestly desired not to meet. That which I greatly feared had at last come upon me. In the Trinity Term of 1929 I gave in, and admitted that God was God, and knelt and prayed: perhaps, that night, the most dejected and reluctant convert in all England. I did not then see what is now the most shining and obvious thing; the Divine humility which will accept and convert even on such terms. The Prodigal Son at least walked home on his own feet. But who can duly adore that Love which will open the high gates to a prodigal who is brought in kicking, struggling, resentful, and darting his eyes in every direction for a chance of escape? The words *compelle intrare*, compel them to come in, have been so abused by wicked men that we shudder at them; but, properly understood, they plumb the depth of the Divine mercy. The hardness of God is kinder that the softness of men, and His compulsion is our liberation."[3]

A certain professor said that in over forty years on campus he had never been asked, "Are you a Christian?" When he was a student he had read books that explained away Christ's miracles; he considered himself well informed and sophisticated on the subject. As a result, on the one hand he disbelieved the deity of Jesus Christ while on the other hand he kept some vague belief in God.

In practice, however, he said, "I usually chose to ignore Him in my early post-college days. This started the path into my own personal wilderness. I tried to satisfy my inner needs by reading and studying literature and science. These studies often confirmed my opinion that I could leave Christ out of my life because He was just another prophet."

Then one day a student entered this professor's "private wilderness" to invite him to hear a campus talk on the deity of Christ. The professor later recalled, "I was confronted with the positive side of Christ's deity for the first time since I was a child. I didn't expect to have my disbelief in the deity of Christ changed.

"As I listened that evening, partly in scepticism, partly in hope, I admit I also yearned to be convinced. The speaker had scarcely completed half of his remarks before I was convinced of the deity of Christ. A lifetime's assumption that Jesus was just another gifted teacher was destroyed. The turnabout in my convictions was simple."

I must agree with the professor. It is simple. Jesus is God. Our earthly lives and eternal destinies depend on our belief in that fact.

8

What Happened at the Cross

IN JEWELLERY STORES from Fifth Avenue to the airport in Rome one piece of jewellery is universally displayed—the cross. Clerical robes have this emblem sewn on the front or back. Churches display the cross in wood, bronze, concrete, or brass. The last month of the year some office buildings light certain windows at night to form a cross which can be seen for miles.

What does the cross of Jesus mean? If we stopped people on the street and asked that question we might hear, "It's a symbol for Christianity, I guess." Or, "Jesus was a martyr and was nailed to a cross." Others might say it was a myth, or a history major might say it was an example of Roman justice.

Another answer to the question "What does the cross mean?" was given by the poet Thomas Victoria. He tried to express how Jesus Himself might speak of the cross if we asked Him. The poet pictured Jesus on the cross, surrounded by men who were intent upon killing Him.

Jesus looks at them and says:

> Oh, how sweet the wood of the cross,
> How sweet the nails,
> That I could die for you.

This deeply personal, intimate view of the cross is what the Apostle Paul taught when he said, "In human experience it is a rare thing for one man to give his life for another, ... though there have been a few who have had the courage to do it. Yet the proof of God's amazing love is this: that it was *while we were sinners* that Christ died for us" (Rom. 5:7, 8, Phillips).

The focus of Paul's whole ministry to the great commercial city of Corinth was summed up when he said, "For I determined to know nothing among you except Jesus Christ, and Him crucified" (1 Cor. 2:2).

The average person in Corinth would have answered a question about the cross in the same way as the man on the street in the USA or any European, African, or Asian country. Corinthians lived in a city which was known for its depraved moral character. It was the kind of town in which we wouldn't want to raise our families. The Corinthians were a sophisticated, sexually dissolute bunch, who thought that the cross was ridiculous, foolish, and even idiotic. Commenting on this view, Paul said, "The foolishness of God is wiser than men, and the weakness of God is stronger than men" (1 Cor. 1:25).

In Corinth the preaching of the cross of Christ was a stumbling block to the Jews, and idiocy to the philosophic Greeks. The philosophers believed they could unravel divine mysteries because they were overconfident of their own mental capacities. However, Paul said that the natural man (meaning the man who does not have the Spirit of God dwelling in him) cannot understand the things of God. He meant that sin has twisted our understanding of truth so that we cannot recognise the truth about God.

Before the teaching in the Bible about the cross can mean anything to us, the Spirit of God must open our minds. The

Scriptures teach that a veil covers our minds as a result of our separation from God.

To an "outsider" the cross must appear to be ridiculous. But to those who have experienced its transforming power, it has become the only remedy for the ills of each person, and of the world.

In spite of this available power, the gospel about Christ who was crucified is still unimportant to millions. They reflect the failure Paul analysed when he questioned; "What have the philosopher, the writer and the critic of this world to show for all their wisdom? Has not God made the wisdom of this world look foolish? For it was after the world in its wisdom had failed to know God, that he in his wisdom chose to save all who would believe by the 'simplemindedness' of the gospel message" (1 Cor. 1:20, 21, Phillips).

How can we brand the message of the cross as foolishness? Have we done so well with our private lives, with our families, and with our society that we can claim wisdom? It's time we abandoned the pretence of being intellectual and recognised that our best minds are baffled by life.

God successfully changes men and women by the message that centres in the cross. His approach recognises our disease and presents the right medicine. He offers His wisdom as an alternative to our failures.

In our everyday life we profit from many helps that we can't understand. We go to the sink and turn on the water tap, never stopping to figure out the source of the water, or how it was carried through the pipes to us. What about a prescription from a doctor? We can't read it or analyse it. We pay a sum we may think is too much because we rely on the doctor's knowledge and authority to make us well.

In the same way we may not be able fully to comprehend the deep significance of the cross, but we can benefit from it because the Bible gives us the authoritative answer to the problem of sin.

WHAT HAPPENED AT THE CROSS?

The cross is the focal point in the life and ministry of Jesus Christ. Some think that God didn't want Christ to die, but was forced to adjust His plans to adapt to it. Scripture makes it very clear, however, that the cross was no afterthought with God. Christ was "delivered up by the predetermined plan and fore-knowledge of God" (Acts 2:23).

God designed the cross to defeat Satan, who by deception had obtained squatter's rights to the title deed of the world. When Satan with all of his clever promises separated man from God in the Garden of Eden, he was more than the deceiver of Adam and Eve. In some mysterious manner he began to exert a kind of pseudosovereignty over man. In his arrogant violence, Satan unleashed his fiercest attack to stop Christ's ministry by seeing that He was murdered. But Satan was stopped by God and caught in his own trap. He hadn't realised that God loved the world so intensely that He could let His own Son be subjected to the worst Satan could do. Satan miscalculated. He didn't comprehend the greatness of God's love and the wisdom of His plan.

Satan's power was broken at the cross. "The Son of God appeared for this purpose, that He might destroy the works of the devil" (1 John 3:8).

What a blow was dealt to Satan! Although he is still a wily pretender, his destruction was made certain by the victory of Christ at the cross. "That through death he might render powerless him who had the power of death, that is, the devil" (Heb. 2:14). What seemed to be the biggest defeat of history turned into the greatest triumph.

Through the cross, God not only overpowered Satan but brought Himself and man together. Christ rescued the slaves that Satan held captive and reconciled them to Himself. The Bible describes this amazing divine plan in these words: "We speak God's wisdom in a mystery, the hidden wisdom, which God predestined before the ages to our glory; the wisdom which none of the rulers of this age has understood; for if they had understood it, they would not have crucified the Lord of Glory" (1 Cor. 2:7, 8).

The cross revealed an eternal secret. This was "the mystery which has been kept secret for long ages past, but now is manifested" (Rom. 16:25, 26).

It it were possible for one man, Adam, to lead mankind to ruin, why shouldn't it be possible for one man to redeem it? The Bible says, "For as in Adam all die, so also in Christ all shall be made alive" (1 Cor. 15:22).

WHAT DID THE CROSS COST GOD?

As human beings filled with our own hurts and desires and emotions, we find it almost impossible to stretch our minds enough to conceive the cost to God in allowing His only Son to go to the cross. If He could have forgiven our sins by any other method, if the problems of the world could have been solved in any other way, God would not have allowed Jesus to die.

In the garden of Gethsemane on the night before He was killed, Jesus prayed, "My Father, if it is possible, let this cup pass from Me" (Matt. 26:39), in other words, if there is any other way to redeem the human race, Oh God, find it! There was no other way. And then He prayed, "Not as I will, but as Thou wilt" (Matt. 26:39).

It's important to understand that when Jesus prayed that prayer, He was not just considering the simple act of dying. Just as His life was unique, so was His death. What happened to Him when He died had never happened to any person in the past and would never happen to anyone in the future. To be able to understand this we need to look into God's revelation before Christ's earthly ministry, back to the Old Testament.

The orthodox Jewish religion was founded on God's grace.

God entered into a convenant relationship with Israel, declaring Himself to be their God and stating in a special way that they were to be His people (Deut. 7:6). With this type of relationship, how were they to express their love for Him? The answer was by doing His will as it was described in the Old Testament law. But the people could not keep the law perfectly, and when they broke it, they sinned. As the Bible says, "Sin is the transgression of the law" (1 John 3:4, AV).

The sacrifices in the temple were meant by God to show graphically that a person's guilt and penalty for sin could be transferred from him to another. In the case of the Old Testament, a perfect animal symbolically bore the penalty and was killed.

Why did God give the law if He knew people couldn't possibly keep it? The Bible teaches that the law was given as a mirror. When we look into it, we see what true righteousness is. The Ten Commandments describe the life that pleases God. If we are separated from God by sin, the law exposes our sin and faces us with our true spiritual condition. The mirror does not reveal a very attractive image!

Sin had to be paid for, so in the beginning God instituted the sacrificial system by which we finally could be brought into a right relationship with God. In Old Testament times, those who had sinned brought sacrifices of animals and offered them to God. These sacrifices were shadows of The Great Sacrifice who was yet to come.

In Leviticus 4, Moses describes a situation in which a leader needs to offer a sacrifice. We can think of it in seven steps:

1. "When a leader sins ...
2. he shall bring for his offering a goat,
3. a male without defect
4. And he shall lay his hand on the head of the male goat
5. and slay it ... ; it is a sin offering.
6. Then the priest is to take some of the blood of the sin offering ... and put it on the horns of the altar....
7. Thus the priest shall make atonement for him in regard to

his sin, and he shall be forgiven" (vv. 22–26).

Notice the sequence. Man sinned and wants forgiveness of God. He brings an animal, a perfect specimen, to the priest and lays his hand on its head. Symbolically, at that point the guilt and punishment he bears because of his sin pass to the animal. He then kills it as a sin offering, and the priest places some of the blood on the altar.

What is the significance? It is an atonement for the man in regard to his sin. In place of a broken relationship between God and the sinner, "atonement" results and "he shall be forgiven" by God.

The sacrifices were visual aids to show sinners that there was hope because the punishment for sin could be transferred to another. However, they were only symbols, because, "It is impossible for the blood of bulls and goats to take away sins" (Heb. 10:4). But God could forgive them in the light of what He would one day do at the cross. Jesus, "having offered one sacrifice for sins for all time, sat down at the right hand of God" (Heb. 10:12).

God did not initiate the sacrifices because He was blood-thirsty or unjust. He wanted us to zero in on two things: first, the loathsomeness of sin, and second, the cross on which God Himself would satisfy forever the demands of His justice. "Not through the blood of goats and calves, but through His own blood He [Jesus] entered the holy place once for all, having obtained eternal redemption" (Heb. 9:12).

When Christ atoned for sin, He stood in the place of guilty men and women. If God had forgiven sin by a divine decree, issuing some sort of a heavenly document written across the sky, without the atonement which involved the personal shame, agony, suffering, and death of Christ, then we might assume that God was indifferent to sin. Consequently we would all go on sinning, and the earth would become a living hell.

In the suffering of Jesus we have the participation of God in the act of atonement. Sin pierced God's heart. God felt every searing

nail and spear. God felt the burning sun. God felt the scorn of His
tormentors and the body blows. In the cross is the suffering love
of God bearing the guilt of man's sin. This love alone is able to
melt the sinner's heart and bring him to repentance for salvation.
"He [God the Father] made Him who knew no sin [Jesus] to be sin
on our behalf" (2 Cor. 5:21).

THE REASON FOR COMMUNION

Many people do not understand communion. For them, the
communion service has no mystical meaning. And yet the cross is
what communion is all about. In the Lord's Supper, Jesus likens
Himself to the Lamb that was offered in the sacrifice or atonement
and says to His disciples and to all who will believe in Him, "This
is my body broken for you." This is symbolic of what He did on
the cross. When the cup is offered the emphasis is upon the fact
that His blood is shed for the remission of sins. The elements of
bread and wine convey to us the reality of atonement and
forgiveness. We can touch them, taste them and see them. We
have bread in our hands, but we have Christ in our hearts. We
have the cup in our hand, but we have the benefits of forgiveness
through His blood in our hearts.

One of the most famous Scottish theologians was John Duncan
of New College in Edinburgh. As communion was being held in
a Church of Scotland on one occasion, when the elements came
to a little sixteen-year-old girl, she suddenly turned her head
aside. She motioned for the elder to take the cup away—that she
couldn't drink it. John Duncan reached his long arm over,
touched her shoulder, and said tenderly, "Take it, lassie, it's for
sinners!"

HOW CAN I UNDERSTAND ALL THIS?

There is a mystery to the death of Christ that is beyond our
human understanding. The depths of God's love in sending His

Son to pay such an awful price is beyond the measure of the mind of man. But we must accept it on faith or we will continually bear the burdens of guilt. We must accept the atonement which Christ has made to try to make our own atonement, and this we can never do. Salvation is by Christ alone through faith alone, and for the glory of God alone.

Christ took the punishment which was due to us.

My friend and associate, Cliff Barrows, told me this story about bearing punishment. He recalled the time when he took the punishment for his children when they had disobeyed. "They had done something I had forbidden them to do. I told them if they did the same thing again I would have to discipline them. When I returned from work and found that they hadn't minded me, the heart went out of me. I just couldn't discipline them."

Any loving father can understand Cliff's dilemma. Most of us have been in the same position. He continued with the story: "Bobby and Bettie Ruth were very small. I called them into my room, took off my belt and my shirt, and with a bare back, knelt down at the bed. I made them both strap me with the belt ten times each. You should have heard the crying! From them, I mean! They didn't want to do it. But I told them the penalty had to be paid and so through their sobs and tears they did what I told them."

Cliff smiled when he remembered the incident. "I must admit I wasn't much of a hero. It hurt. I haven't offered to do that again, but I never had to spank them again, either, because they got the point. We kissed each other when it was over and prayed together."

In that infinite way that staggers our hearts and minds, we know that Christ paid the penalty for our sins, past, present, and future.

That is why He died on the cross.

9

The King's Courtroom

THE UNITED STATES has a presidential election every four years. Changes are usually made in the White House, the Congress, and in many governors' mansions. When one elected leader is about to step down for his successor, he may grant some pardons to prisoners under his jurisdiction. It's always interesting to see who might benefit from these last-minute gestures.

If you or I were in prison and were told, "You're free. The president just granted you a pardon," we would certainly pack up and get out fast! That pardon would change our lives.

In the courtroom of the King of kings, a pardon means much more. At the cross, God not only delivered the believer in Christ from punishment, He also welcomed him with open arms into His family. He opens His home to us.

At the cross we have not only acquittal, but also justification (just-as-if-I'd-never-sinned); not only pardon, but also acceptance. We saw in the last chapter that God Himself bore the burden of our sin and suffered for us. Now we must see that the cross offers us more than a pardon.

The issue involved is not just in Jesus' blood, which cleanses us from sin, but also in His righteousness. The key is in the word "justified." We are "justified as a gift by His grace through the redemption which is in Christ Jesus" (Rom. 3:24).

Several years ago I was to be interviewed at my home for a well-known television show and, knowing that it would appear on nationwide television, my wife took great pains to see that everything looked nice. She had vacuumed and dusted and tidied up the whole house but had gone over the living room with a fine-tooth comb since that was where the interview would be filmed. When the film crew arrived with all the lights and cameras, she felt that everything in that living room was spic and span. We were in place along with the interviewer when suddenly the television lights were turned on and we saw cobwebs and dust where we had never seen them before. In the words of my wife: "I mean, that room was festooned with dust and cobwebs which simply did not show up under ordinary light."

The point is, of course, that no matter how well we clean up our lives and think we have them all in order, when we see ourselves in the light of God's Word, in the light of God's holiness, all the cobwebs and all the dust do show up.

Picture a courtroom. God the Judge is seated in the judge's seat, robed in splendour. You are arraigned before Him. He looks at you in terms of His own righteous nature as it is expressed in the moral law. He speaks to you:

GOD: John (or) Mary, have you loved Me with all your heart?

JOHN/MARY: No, Your Honour.

GOD: Have you loved others as you have loved yourself?

JOHN/MARY: No, Your Honour.

GOD: Do you believe you are a sinner and that Jesus Christ died for your sins?

JOHN/MARY: Yes, Your Honour.

GOD: Then your penalty has been paid by Jesus Christ on the cross and you are pardoned.

I have my pardon, but there is much more. When the Bible says that the person who believes in Jesus is justified as a gift by His grace (see Rom. 3:24), this sounds like more than a mere pardon. And it is. If I'm a criminal whom the president or the governor pardons, everyone knows I'm still guilty. I simply don't have to serve my sentence. But if I'm justified, it's *just-as-if-I'd* never sinned at all.

Both pardon and justification come to us when we believe in Jesus. On the one hand God pardons our sin because of the death of Christ. He paid our penalty. On the other hand God actually declares us "righteous" (a word which means the same as "just").

GOD: Because Christ is righteous, and you believe in Christ, I now declare you legally righteous.

How can God do that and remain "just" Himself — when He attached the penalty of death to sin? The answer is in the righteousness of Jesus Christ. He lived an unblemished, perfect life. His character perfectly supported His claim to deity, as we saw in chapter 7, "The Man Who Is God." It's easy to see God the Father declaring Jesus just, because He was. But how does that help me, a sinner? Paul gives the answer in 2 Corinthians 5:21. To make it clear we'll substitute the words *God* and *Christ* where the words *He* and *Him* appear. "God made Christ who knew no sin to be sin on our behalf, that we might become the righteousness of God in Christ."

God put my sin on Christ, who had no sin; He punished Him in my place, as we have seen. But He did one other thing, according to this verse. By God's action the righteousness of Christ was put on us who believe, "that we might become the righteousness of God in Him."

The Judge, God, has transferred Christ's righteousness to your legal account if you have believed in Christ. Now He examines you according to law. What does He see? All of your past evil deeds and thoughts? Your sinful actions of the present? No. He doesn't see your sin because that has been transferred to Christ when God made Christ to be sin. Rather He looks at you carefully and sees the righteousness of Christ.

But you may say, "Look, am I not still a sinful person?"

The answer is "Yes and No." If you mean that you have the legal status of a sinner before God, the answer is "No." To Him, legally, you are just. You are in right standing before Him, and "standing" is the issue in the courtroom.

Do you still have the capacity to sin? The answer is "Yes." Of course you are not perfect. You may still at times think and act in ways contrary to God's desires. But your character and mine aren't the issue here. Our legal standing is. And legally we are declared just.

AM I FREE TO SIN?

"Love God and live as you please!" Now are we free to sin without restraint? Can we run out of the courtroom, pardoned and justified, and do anything we want? Yes. But you are now "born again." You don't want to do the same old wrong things; your desires are changed.

If you have trusted Jesus and seen what depth of concern He had for you at the cross, you can say with the Apostle Paul, "It is Christ's love that controls me" (2 Cor. 5:14, Goodspeed). The inner changes God begins to achieve in our character will be the subject of a later chapter. But they are all based on a change in status. We who were properly condemned are now properly declared just if we have trusted Christ.

Can you imagine what a newspaper man would do with this event?

SINNER PARDONED—GOES
TO LIVE WITH JUDGE

It was a tense scene when John and Mary stood before the Judge and had the list of charges against them read. However, the

Judge transferred all of the guilt to Jesus Christ, who died on a cross for John and Mary.

After John and Mary were pardoned the Judge invited them to come to live with Him forever.

The reporter on a story like that would never be able to understand the irony of such a scene, unless he had been introduced to the Judge beforehand and knew His character.

Pardon and Christ's righteousness come to us only when we totally trust ourselves to Jesus as our Lord and Saviour. When we do this, God welcomes us into His intimate favour. Clothed in Christ's righteousness we can now enjoy God's fellowship and "come boldly unto the throne of grace, that we may obtain mercy, and find grace to help in time of need" (Heb. 4:16, AV).

CONCLUSIONS FROM THE TESTIMONY

If I were a lawyer, I'm sure I would study the procedures of great trials of the past, the evidences presented, and the conclusions reached by the findings.

There are some vital conclusions we can draw from the death of Christ. First, at the cross we see the strongest evidence of the guilt of the world. Here sin reached its climax when its terrible display occurred. Sin was never blacker or more hideous than on the day Christ died.

Some people have said that man has improved since then and that if Christ returned today He wouldn't be crucified but might even be given a glorious reception. I am convinced that if Christ came today He might be tortured and put to death even more quickly than He was two thousand years ago, though perhaps in different, more sophisticated ways. But sinful people would still shout, "Away with Him."

Human sinful nature has not changed. As we look at the cross we see clear proof that all men have "sinned and fallen short of the glory of God." This is God's inescapable verdict.

The second conclusion we see at the cross is that God hates sin and loves righteousness. He has told us repeatedly that the soul that sins shall die, and that He cannot forgive our sin unless our debt has been paid. The Scripture says, "Without the shedding of blood there is no forgiveness of sins" (Heb. 9:22, RSV).

God will not tolerate sin. As the moral judge of the entire universe, He cannot compromise if He is to remain just. His holiness and His justice demand the penalty for broken law. There are some schools of thought which feel that such a view of God is too severe. Sin, they say, has its psychological basis. Some time ago a young man was executed for killing two other young men. The newspapers were full of the legal arguments, the debates over the death penalty, and the frequent postponements of the execution date. Why did he do it? What events or people in his past influenced his twisted mind?

Many say they are not responsible for what they do. Poor parents, bad environment, the government are all blamed. But God says that we are responsible. When we look at the cross, we see how drastically God deals with sin. The Bible says, "He who did not spare His own Son, but delivered Him up for us all, how will He not also with Him freely give us all things?" (Rom. 8:32). "For our sake He [God] made Him [Christ] to be sin who knew no sin" (2 Cor. 5:21, RSV).

If God had to send His only Son to the cross to pay the penalty for sin, then sin must be terrible indeed in His sight.

However, we see that God loves righteousness and clothes the believer in His righteousness because of the cross. It is amazing to think about! We are clothed, we are covered, protected, shielded. A wonderful old hymn says, "Jesus, thy blood and righteousness, My beauty are, my glorious dress."[1] This is not self-righteousness, but "the righteousness which comes from God on the basis of faith" (Phil. 3:9).

God is now at work through the Holy Spirit to make the believer righteous in his inner character. Peter shows how intimately this is based on the cross also when he says of Christ that "He Himself bore our sins in His body on the cross, that we might die to sin and live to righteousness" (1 Pet. 2:24).

What other conclusion must we reach from the testimony of the cross? We see the greatest demonstration of God's love. "For God so loved the world, that He gave His only begotten Son, that whoever believes in Him should not perish, but have eternal life" (John 3:16).

In our own weakness as humans, we tend to grade sins. Here's a little sin on our scale, but over here there's a very, very heavy sin. We may see God as able to forgive the small sin, but incapable of forgiving and accepting the gross sinner. I recall a story out of World War II that illustrates this graphically. Hitler and his Third Reich had gone down to defeat at the hands of the Allies. Many of the men who had been Nazi leaders in some of the most infamous crimes known to man were brought to trial in Nuremberg. The world watched as sentences of imprisonment and death were brought against these war criminals.

However, out of the Nuremberg trials came an amazing account by Chaplain Henry Gerecke. He was called upon to be prison chaplain to the former Nazi high command. He described himself as a humble preacher, a one-time Missouri farm boy, and then he was given this extremely difficult assignment.

Chaplain Gerecke recalls the sincere conversion to faith in Jesus Christ by some of these men who had committed despicable crimes. One of them was a former favourite general of Hitler. At first the chaplain was very leery of confessions of faith. He said the first time he saw this criminal reading his Bible he thought, "a phony." However, as he spent time with him he wrote, "But the longer I listened, the more I felt he might be sincere. He said he had not been a good Christian. He insisted he was very glad that a nation which would probably put him to death thought enough of his eternal welfare to provide him with spiritual guidance." With his Bible in his hand he said, "I know from this book that God can love a sinner like me."[2]

What an amazing love God exhibited for us at the cross!

The fourth conclusion we can reach from the testimony at the cross is that it is the basis for true world brotherhood. There are many groups which espouse the brotherhood of man and make appeals in behalf of peace. Only when we are brought into the family of God through the Fatherhood of God can there be any true brotherhood of man. God is not our Father automatically (except by creation) when we are born; He must become our Father spiritually.

The Bible teaches that we can experience glorious brotherhood and Fatherhood through the cross. "For He Himself is our peace, who made both groups into one, and broke down the barrier of the dividing wall, by abolishing in His flesh the enmity, which is the Law of commandments contained in ordinances, that in Himself He might make the two into one new man, thus establishing peace" (Eph. 2:14,15).

Outside the work of the cross we see bitterness, intolerance, hatred, prejudice, lust, and greed. Within the powerful working of the cross grow love, new life, and new brotherhood. The only human hope for peace lies at the cross of Christ, where all men, no matter what their background of nationality or race, can become a new brotherhood.

You are probably familiar with the story of Hansi. Her book *Hansi* describes vividly her absolute dedication to Adolph Hitler and the Nazi movement as a member of the Hitler Youth; her subsequent disenchantment and disillusionment; then her conversion to Jesus Christ. My wife has a letter from Hansi telling of her first meeting with Corrie ten Boom, whose book *The Hiding Place* tells of the ten Boom family's experiences during World War II. The family was arrested and put in prison for hiding Jews, and Corrie's father and sister died there.

One day Hansi and Corrie were at a convention and were seated in the same building, autographing their books. Hansi waited as long as she could, then made her way to Corrie because she simply had to ask forgiveness for what she had done. Hansi pushed through those standing in line with their books for Corrie to sign, knelt in front of Corrie with tears streaming down her cheeks and said, "Corrie, I'm Hansi." Corrie's reaction was not only absolute forgiveness, but love and acceptance. This could only happen between Christians and illustrates what the cross does.

Captain Mitsuo Fuchida was the Japanese naval air commander who led the bombing attack on Pearl Harbour. He relates that when the Japanese war prisoners were returning from America he was curious as to what kind of treatment they had received. An ex-prisoner he questioned told him what made it possible for those in the camp to forget their hate and hostility toward their captors. One young girl had been extremely kind and helpful and had shown such love and tenderness for them that their hearts were touched. They wondered why she was so good to them and were amazed when she told them it was because her parents had been killed by the Japanese army! She explained that her parents had been Christian missionaries in the Philippines at the beginning of the war but when the Japanese landed they were forced to flee to the mountains. They were later found by the Japanese, accused of being spies and put to death. But before they were killed they had asked for thirty minutes of time to pray, which was granted. The girl was convinced that her parents had spent that thirty minutes praying for forgiveness for their executioners, and because of this she was able to allow the Holy Spirit to remove the hate from her heart and replace it with love.

Captain Fuchida could not understand such love. Several months passed and one day in Tokyo he was given a leaflet as he left a railroad station. This told the story of Sergeant Jacob DeShazer who was captured by the Japanese, tortured, and held prisoner of war for forty months. While in prison camp he received Christ through reading the Bible. God's Word removed the bitter hatred for the Japanese from his heart and replaced it with such love that he was compelled to return to tell the Japanese people of this marvellous love of Christ.

Captain Fuchida bought a Bible and began to read. He faced the scene of the crucifixion of Christ and was struck by Jesus' words "Father forgive them; for they do not know what they are doing" (Luke 23:34). Jesus prayed for the very soldiers who were about to thrust the spear into His side. In his book *From Pearl Harbour to Golgotha* Captain Fuchida tells how he found the source of this miracle love that can forgive enemies, and how he could now understand the story of the American girl whose parents had been slain and the transformation in Jake DeShazer's life.

PERSONAL QUESTIONS THE CROSS ANSWERS

"Why can't I seem to solve my problems?" This question reminds me of a Peanuts cartoon. It pictures Lucy in her psychiatrist's booth giving counsel to Charlie Brown. Charlie has lost another ball game and feels depressed and defeated. Lucy, the psychiatrist, is explaining to him that life is made of ups and downs. Charlie goes away screaming, "But I hate downs, all I want is ups."

I'm afraid that often those of us who teach the Christian message give the impression that once we have accepted Jesus Christ we will never again have any problems. This isn't true, but we do have Someone to help us face our problems. I have a friend who has been a paraplegic for over thirty years. In spite of overwhelming problems for which there is no solution, she has learned not only to live with her condition, but to be radiant and triumphant, blessing and winning others to Christ.

Paul Tournier, one of the great Swiss psychiatrists, has stated that in the Christian life we have to realise that each day will present new circumstances and there will always be adjustments that have to be made. If I drive my car into a city, I can't rigidly place my hands on the steering wheel and drive at a set rate of speed. I have to stop and start and turn to make adjustments. The same thing is true in daily living. There is always a price to being a person; part of that price is pain and problems, but we have the promise Christ made that He will always be with us.

In Psalm 34 there are three great statements about our problems:

"This poor man cried and the Lord heard him; and saved him out of all his troubles" (v. 6).

"The righteous cry and the Lord hears, and delivers them out of all their troubles" (v. 17).

"Many are the afflictions of the righteous; but the Lord delivers him out of them all" (v. 19).

The Christian life is not a way "out" but a way "through" life. The "out of" in these verses refers to deliverance not from but through difficulty. The English scholar Dr. Arthur Way phrased it, "deliverance out of, not from the crisis of trial. So that the sense appears to be, 'bring me safely out of the conflict' " and, "not simply keep me from entering into it."

Another question: "I feel so guilty—how can I find relief?"

Guilt is a very debilitating feeling. It can destroy our attitude, our personal relationships, and our outreach. Sometimes we feel guilty because we've done things that are wrong for which we must accept the responsibility and also accept God's forgiveness.

I have been told by doctors that a large percentage of the patients in psychiatric hospitals could be released if only they could be assured of the fact that they had been forgiven.

It's so easy to blame someone or something else. Anna Russell, the British comedienne, has an interesting little poem about guilt entitled "Jolly Old Sigmund Freud":

I went to my psychiatrist to be psychoanalysed.
To find out why I kicked the cat, and blacked my wifey's eyes.
He laid me on his downy couch to see what he could find,
And this is what he dredged up from my subconscious mind.

When I was one my mama hid my dolly in a trunk,
And so it falls naturally that I am always drunk.
When I was two I suffered from ambivalence toward my
   brothers,
And so it falls naturally I poisoned all my lovers.
Now I am so glad that I have learned the lessons this has
   taught,
That everything I do that's wrong is someone else's fault. *

For some people guilt is an excuse. They won't accept the
forgiveness that is offered to them; it is so hard to believe. It seems
too good to be true that God should let us go eternally scot-free
from our sins—and yet that is the message that the gospel brings
to us. When we cling to our guilt we do not honour God and we
handicap our own lives terribly.

Forgiveness is an opportunity that Christ extended to us on the
cross. When we accept His forgiveness and are willing to forgive
ourselves, then we find relief.

After the sewage plants of London have reclaimed all that is
usable of sewage, sludge barges on the river Thames collect the
residue and carry it out to sea a certain number of miles and
dump it. Apparently it is only a matter of minutes before the sea
water is as pure as it was before! This is a beautiful illustration of
how He has buried our sins in the depths of the sea.

Corrie ten Boom tells a story of a little girl who broke one of
her mother's treasured demitasse cups. The little girl came to her
mother sobbing, "Oh, mama, I'm so sorry I broke your beautiful
cup."

The mother replied, "I know you're sorry and I forgive you.
Now don't cry any more." The mother then swept up the pieces
of the broken cup and placed them in the trash can. But the little
girl enjoyed the guilty feeling. She went to the trash can, picked

---

* From *The Anna Russell Song Book*. Reprinted by permission of Citadel Press, Division
of Lyle Stuart, Inc., 120 Enterprise Ave., Secaucus, N.J. 07094.

out pieces of the cup, brought them to her mother and sobbed, "Mother, I'm so sorry that I broke your pretty cup."

This time her mother spoke firmly to her, "Take those pieces and put them back in the trash can and don't be silly enough to take them out again. I told you I forgave you so don't cry any more, and don't pick up the broken pieces any more."

Guilt is removed with confession and cleansing. "If we confess our sins, He is faithful and just to forgive us our sins, and to cleanse us from all unrighteousness" (1 John 1:9, AV).

However, the story of David's sin (Ps. 51) shows that forgiveness does not preclude the natural consequences of our sin. Murder can be forgiven, but that does not bring the dead to life again.

There is a well-known story of some men in Scotland who had spent the day fishing. That evening they were having tea in a little inn. One of the fishermen, in a characteristic gesture to describe the size of the fish that got away, flung out his hands just as the little waitress was getting ready to set the cup of tea at his place. The hand and the teacup collided, dashing the tea against the whitewashed walls. Immediately an ugly brown stain began to spread over the wall. The man who did it was very embarrassed and apologised profusely, but one of the other guests jumped up and said, "Never mind." Pulling a pen from his pocket, he began to sketch around the ugly brown stain. Soon there emerged a picture of a magnificent royal stag with his antlers spread. That artist was Sir Edwin Landseer, England's foremost painter of animals.

This story has always beautifully illustrated to me the fact that if we confess not only our sins but our mistakes to God, He can make out of them something for our good and for His glory. Somehow it's harder to commit our mistakes and stupidities to God than it is our sins. Mistakes and stupidities seem so dumb, whereas sin seems more or less to be an outcropping of our human nature. But Romans 8:28 tells us that if they are committed to God He can make them work together for our good and His glory.

When you bake a cake, you put in raw flour, baking powder, soda, bitter chocolate, shortening, etc., none of which taste very good in themselves, but which work together to make a delicious cake. And so with our sins and our mistakes—although they are not good in themselves, if we commit them in honest, simple faith to the Lord, He will work them out His own way and in His own time make something of them for our good and His glory.

Question: "Do I have to understand all this about Christ's death?"

The depths of God's love in sending His son to pay such an awful price is beyond the measure of the mind of man. We must accept it on faith or we will continually bear the burden of guilt. Salvation is by Christ alone, through faith alone, for the glory of God alone.

Jesus never said, "Only understand." He said, "Only believe."

10

Jesus Christ Is Alive

IN A MAUSOLEUM in Moscow's Red Square lie the embalmed remains of Lenin. A crystal casket in that tomb has been viewed by millions of people. On the casket it says: "For he was the greatest leader of all people of all time. He was the lord of the new humanity; he was the saviour of the world."

The tribute to Lenin is stated in the past tense. What a startling contrast to the triumphant words of Christ. "I am the resurrection, and the life; he who believes in Me shall live even if he dies" (John 11:25).

The basis for our belief in Jesus Christ is in His resurrection. Karl Barth, the great Swiss theologian, said that without belief in the physical resurrection of Jesus Christ there is no salvation.

If Christ were entombed somewhere in a grave near Jerusalem where the millions who visit Israel each year could walk by a grave and worship Him, then Christianity would be a fable. The Apostle Paul said, "If Christ has not been raised, then our preaching is in vain and your faith is in vain.... If Christ has not been raised, your faith is futile and you are still in your sins" (1 Cor. 15:14,17, RSV).

We usually hear a sermon about the resurrection every Easter, and that's about all. But when the early apostles preached, the cross and resurrection were their constant themes. Without the resurrection, the cross is meaningless.

SHALL MAN LIVE AGAIN?

Some say we are nothing but bone, flesh, and blood. After we have died, nothing happens—we don't go anywhere. Or if we do go somewhere it is to a nebulous location, devised by the imagination to represent almost anything.

Does science help? I have questioned scientists concerning life after death and most of them say, "We just don't know." Science deals in formulas and test tubes; the spiritual world is beyond its reach.

Many who do not believe in life after death fill their writings with tragedy and pessimism. Gore Vidal, Truman Capote, Dalton Trumbo, and many others write with almost unrelieved pessimism. How different are the words of Jesus Christ, who said, "Because I live, you shall live also" (John 14:19). We must base our hope of immortality on Christ alone—not on any longings, arguments, or instinctive feelings of immortality.

The Bible speaks of the resurrection of Jesus as something which could be examined by the physical senses. The disciples saw Him under many different conditions after He had been raised. A single disciple saw Him on one occasion, five hundred on another. Some saw Jesus separately, some together; some for a moment, some for a long time.

The disciples heard Him in conversation. They were told to touch Him to verify His physical reality. They touched Him, walked with Him, conversed with Him, ate with Him, and examined Him. This took the resurrection appearances of Jesus out of the realm of hallucination and put them into the realm of demonstrable physical fact.

Historical fact provides the basis for our belief in the bodily resurrection of Christ. We have more evidence for it than for any other event of that time, secular or religious.

WHAT ABOUT THE OTHER RELIGIONS?

Most of the world religions are based upon philosophical thought, except for Judaism, Buddhism, Islam, and Christianity. These four are based upon personalities. Only Christianity claims resurrection for its founder.

Abraham, the father of Judaism, died about nineteen centuries before Christ. There are no evidences for his resurrection.

Buddha lived about five centuries before Christ, and taught principles of brotherly love. It is believed that he died at the age of eighty. There are no evidences for his resurrection.

Muhammad died A.D. 632, and his tomb at Medina is visited by thousands of devout Mohammedans. His birthplace at Mecca sees many pilgrims each year. However, there are no evidences for his resurrection.

EVIDENCES OF CHRIST'S RESURRECTION

There is something called "the swoon theory" which says that Jesus didn't actually die, but only fainted. Since there could be no resurrection without a death, this thought denies His resurrection. Yet the evidence for His death is strong.

The soldiers were positive Jesus was dead, so they didn't need to induce death by shock through breaking His legs, which they did to the two thieves beside Him. It was not the friends of Jesus, but His enemies who vouched for His death. Also, they made certain when they thrust a spear into His heart.

One of the wealthiest men in the world, Howard Hughes, died recently. The events and circumstances surrounding his death are still shrouded in mystery, and yet he had an entourage of men who followed and guarded him for years.

In a city in the Middle East, however, there is more historical evidence for the death of one man, alone on a cross between two thieves, than any other in history. The great Bible student Wilbur Smith said, "Let it simply be said that we know more about the details of the hours immediately before, and the actual death of Jesus, in and near Jerusalem, than we know about the death of any other one man in all the ancient world."[1]

Jesus was buried. We know more about the burial of Jesus than we know of the burial of any character in ancient history. His body was taken from the cross and wrapped in fine linen with spices. Joseph of Arimathea, a rich man and a secret disciple of Jesus, mustered up his courage and asked Pilate for the body of Jesus. When his request was granted, we are told, he took Him down from the cross and wrapped Him in a linen sheet (Matt. 27:59). We are told that Nicodemus (the same religious leader who had asked Jesus how to be born again) came and brought a very expensive mixture of myrrh and aloes to wrap in with the linens, as was the custom of Jewish burial.

The body of Jesus was placed in Joseph's own tomb, which was located in the garden. This burial procedure shows that it was the body of Jesus which was buried, not His spirit. Spirits are immaterial and cannot be buried.

After Jesus was buried, a huge stone was placed against the face of the tomb and a seal placed upon that. Anyone trying to move the stone from the entrance to the tomb would have had to break the Roman seal and face the consequences of the harsh Roman law.

To make sure that His disciples didn't steal His body, a Roman guard was then placed in front of the sealed stone. The enemies of Jesus didn't want to take any chances that the prophecy about His resurrection would take place.

What about the Roman guards? These men weren't cowards. Their discipline was so severe that the punishment for quitting their post, or even falling asleep on the job, was death.

Historians say there were probably four guards on watch at the tomb, all of them outfitted with strong weapons and shields. No chances were taken that this Jesus would be removed from the tomb.

The empty tomb. It was the third day, the day Jesus said He would arise. Around the tomb the earth began to shake, and along with it the armour of the Roman soldiers must have clattered wildly. And then an angel of the Lord came from heaven and easily rolled away the stone and sat on it. He didn't even have to say, "Hi, fellas!" The guards just looked at him and became like dead men. The angel spoke to Mary Magdalene and Mary, too, but the Bible says that they took action and ran to tell the disciples that He had risen.

When Peter and John came running to the tomb, John peeped in and saw the linen clothes Christ had been wrapped in lying there empty. Peter, who, true to his character, blundered right in, saw that Jesus' body was missing. He was gone.

The bodily resurrection was a fact attested to by hundreds of eyewitnesses. We have records of thirteen different appearances of Jesus under widely different circumstances. His body was both similar and dissimilar to the one nailed to the cross. It was so similar to an ordinary human body that Mary mistook Him for the caretaker of the garden by the tomb when He appeared to her. He could eat, speak to people, and occupy space.

However, His body was not like a normal body. He could pass through closed doors or vanish in a moment. Christ's body was physical, and also spiritual. Why should this be surprising? Paul said to King Agrippa, "Why should it be thought a thing incredible with you, that God should raise the dead?" (Acts 26:8 AV).

Over and over again the Bible affirms the fact of the bodily resurrection of Christ. Luke says it very directly in the book of Acts. He reports that Jesus "presented Himself alive, after His suffering, by many convincing proofs, appearing to them over a period of forty days" (Acts 1:3).

In speaking about those "convincing proofs," C. S. Lewis says, "The first fact in the history of Christendom is a number of people who say they have seen the Resurrection. If they had died without making anyone else believe this 'gospel' no gospels would ever have been written."[2]

THE RESURRECTION ESSENTIAL

There is a series of events that form links in a chain from eternity to eternity. These include the incarnation of Jesus, His crucifixion, resurrection, ascension, and return. Any missing link and the chain is destroyed.

All of Christianity as a system of truth collapses if the resurrection is rejected. As Paul said, "If Christ has not been raised, then our preaching is vain, your faith also is vain" (1 Cor. 15:14).

In addition to breaking the chain of redemptive events, if the resurrection were not essential, then the good news of salvation would be flat, lifeless, and negative. Resurrection is central to the gospel. Paul said, "Now I make known to you, brethren, the gospel which I preached to you, which also you received, in which also you stand, by which also you are saved, if you hold fast the word which I preached to you, unless you believed in vain. For I delivered to you as of first importance what I also received, that Christ died for our sins according to the Scriptures, and that He was buried, and that He was raised on the third day according to the Scriptures" (1 Cor. 15:1–4).

In my book *World Aflame*, I told the story about Auguste Comte, the French philosopher, and Thomas Carlyle, the Scottish essayist. Comte said he was going to start a new religion that would supplant the religion of Christ. It was to have no mysteries and was to be as plain as the multiplication table; its name was to be positivism. "Very good, Mr. Comte," Carlyle replied, "Very good. All you will need to do will be to speak as never a man spake, and live as never a man lived, and be crucified, and rise again the third day, and get the world t) believe that you are still alive. Then your religion will have a chance to get on."

Today many "new religions" are springing up, like toadstools after a summer rain. I wonder how many could meet the criteria that Carlyle told his friend?

We have been emphasising throughout this book the experience of being born again. A personal salvation experience is directly related to belief in the resurrection. Paul gave the formula for saving faith and showed that it centred in this belief: "If you confess with your mouth Jesus as Lord, and believe in your heart that God raised Him from the dead, you shall be saved; for with the heart man believes, resulting in righteousness, and with the mouth he confesses, resulting in salvation" (Rom. 10:9,10).

It couldn't be clearer in the Scriptures. Yet there are churches where ministers say they believe in the resurrection, but that this means Jesus immediately rose from death into spiritual life with God. They say they believe in a "spiritual" but not a "physical" resurrection. This is what some modern preachers proclaim on Easter morning—though I am thankful they are diminishing in number.

No wonder there are many who sit in some churches week after week, year after year, without hearing the whole gospel and knowing what it is to be born again. They hear a gospel which is incomplete, and consequently not good news at all. The resurrection was not disembodied, it was physical. Eyewitnesses said, "We saw His glory"; "You will see Him"; "He appeared"; "I have seen Jesus the Lord."

Within the short span of three days both events, the death and resurrection, took place bodily and not symbolically—tangibly, not spiritually—watched by men of flesh and blood, not fabricated by hallucination.

The resurrection was also the pledge and the promise of our own resurrection.

To understand this we need to see that, in the Bible, death affects both personality and body. (Remember the three dimensions of death?) The body, too, has to be retrieved from condemnation. Only by resurrecting the body could God make a complete conquest of death. He started with the body of Jesus, but He will also work in a similar manner with the bodies of all who believe. As the judgment of death was total, so salvation from its penalty is total, involving the physical, spiritual, and eternal.

Obviously our resurrection bodies will be recognisable, but they can't possibly be the exact bodies we have here. However, they must be like Christ's resurrected body. He had the nail prints and the wound in His side, and yet He could pass through closed doors. When it was time for Him to go to heaven He was able to ascend.

What a promise this is! "For if we believe that Jesus died and rose again, even so God will bring with Him those who have fallen asleep in Jesus" (1 Thess. 4:14).

Jesus staked everything upon His rising from the dead. By His resurrection He would be judged true or false.

WHAT DOES THE RESURRECTION MEAN TO US TODAY?

Christ lives with every person who puts his trust in Him. The resurrection means the presence of the living Christ. He said, "Lo, I am with you alway, even unto the end of the world" (Matt. 28:20, AV). This is Christ's own guarantee: life has a new meaning. After the crucifixion, the disciples were in despair. They said, "We had hoped that he was the one to redeem Israel" (Luke 24:21, RSV). They were full of anguish because they thought of Christ's death as such a tragedy. Life had lost its meaning for them. But when He rose from the grave, they saw the living Christ; and life took on purpose once more.

We can also claim the prayers of the living Christ. The Bible says, "Christ Jesus is He who died, yes, rather who was raised, who is at the right hand of God, who also intercedes for us" (Rom. 8:34). We don't have to think that our prayers are bouncing off the ceiling. The living Christ is sitting at the right hand of God the Father. God the Son retains the same humanity He took to save us, and is now living in a body that still has nail prints in its hands. He is our great High Priest, interceding for us with God the Father.

The resurrection presence of Christ gives us power to live our lives day by day and to serve Him. "Truly, truly, I say to you, he who believes in Me, the works that I do shall he do also; and greater works than these shall he do; because I go to the Father" (John 14:12).

The resurrected body of Jesus is the design for our bodies when we are raised from the dead also. No matter what afflictions, pain, or distortions we have in our earthly bodies, we will be given new bodies. What a glorious promise of things to come! "For our citizenship is in heaven, from which also we eagerly wait for a Saviour, the Lord Jesus Christ; who will transform the body of our humble state into conformity with the body of His glory, by the exertion of the power that He has even to subject all things to Himself" (Phil. 3:20,21).

Thousands of people today are excited about Bible prophecy. The revelation of what the Bible says about events, past, present, and future, has become more prominent in the themes of books, sermons, and conferences. The Second Coming of Christ is becoming a closer and closer reality for those of us who study the Bible and the world scene.

The entire plan for the future has its key in the resurrection. Unless Christ was raised from the dead, there can be no kingdom and no returning King. When the disciples stood at the place Jesus left this earth, which is called the place of ascension, they were given assurance by angels that the Christ of resurrection would be the Christ of returning glory. "Men of Galilee, why do you stand looking into the sky? This Jesus, who has been taken up from you into heaven, will come in just the same way as you have watched Him go into heaven" (Acts 1:11).

The resurrection is an event which prepares us and confirms for us that future event when He will return again.

Yes, Jesus Christ is alive.

Obviously Christ's physical resurrection is an essential part of God's plan to save us. Have you given yourself to this living Christ?

A woman wrote us this: "Last evening I was alone and watching television. I had no *TV Guide*. Something urged me to turn the dial to the station where the gospel was being preached. I had been really wrestling with a great problem. I was and am facing death, and may or may not be helped through surgery. I had been putting off the operation because I was afraid I had been cut off from God.

"I began to really seek the Lord. The message I heard was God's way of speaking to me and answering my prayers. Now I feel entirely at peace in my soul."

If you trust the resurrected Christ as your Lord and Saviour, He will be with you when you die, and will give you life with Him forever. Because of the resurrection, you can be "Born Again."

III

Man's Response

11

The New Birth Is for Now

THE COFFEE SEEMS bitter and the toast cold when the morning newspaper is finished. Another riot in Egypt. Africa torn apart by rival factions. The Middle East seemed quiet until another border incident set off new hostilities. Three coeds murdered on the campus of a prominent state university.

What can the average person do? He feels inadequate, powerless. All of the committees, the resolutions, the changes in governments don't seem to change society.

We see that if mankind is to be saved, something radical needs to be done quickly. The forces building up in our world are so overwhelming that men and women everywhere are beginning to cry out in desperation. They feel like the man John Bunyan describes in the beginning of *Pilgrim's Progress*. " ... he was greatly distressed in his mind, he burst out, as he had done before, crying, 'What shall I do to be saved?' "

So much in our world seems to improve, but man doesn't. We can send a spaceship to the moon and take close-up pictures of

Mars, but we can't walk safely on the streets at night. The subtle sins of selfishness and indifference are everywhere. Seemingly upright men and women admit to desires of the grossest sort. (And who is shocked any more?) Human viciousness breaks out as people steal, cheat, lie, murder, and rape.

Someone in the movie industry said that all we would have to do is contrast the titles of some of the old movie classics with current movie offerings to see the change in morality during the past generation. It's a long way from *Desert Song* to *Deep Throat*.

Man has made many attempts to change himself. We have tried without success to achieve moral goals by improvement in our environment and many are disillusioned with the results.

How can we change human nature?

FROM THE OUTSIDE IN

Studies in anthropology, psychology, and sociology to discover the laws of human behaviour are an important part of educational research. Too often, however, the researchers themselves ignore the fact of human sin and see a human being by his environment. At a meeting of the American Anthropological Association a new discipline was introduced to the academic community by a Harvard zoologist. He calls it "sociobiology," and it is described as "the study of the biological basis for social behaviour in every species; its practitioners believe that some—and perhaps much—of human behaviour is genetically determined."[1]

The sociobiologists imply that "a good deal more of mankind's morality may be genetically based."[2] They fail to give a proper place to the inborn twist toward selfishness, viciousness, and indifference to God, so many of their conclusions are only pseudoscientific.

If we are shaped by our genes, and moulded by our environment, then all we need to do is develop a way to alter genetic bases in humans or cure man's environment in terms of bad housing, slums, poverty, unemployment, and racial discrimination.

A best-selling author said this: "Many ministers today 'keep their cool' about questions of the sin and repentance of individuals and have turned their attack on the sin of society, in an attempt to make society squirm. This 'attack' varies from a mild sociology lecture to an angry assault against social injustice. However, slums and ghettos and put-downs are not going to disappear in society unless slums and games disappear from the hearts of people."[3]

But as Christians we need to do something about social injustice, slums and ghettos. We cannot sit back with the attitude that the problems are too overwhelming or insoluble. We need to get involved in helping to make this world a better place to live for the unfortunate whose standard of living is so low as to defy imagination, and for those who live under terrible political oppression. Ultimately, however, society is not going to be changed with coercion and force because when it is changed that way, man usually loses his freedom. It can be changed only by a complete transformation of the human heart.

Man also attempts to change himself by *chemistry*. Scientists have developed methods to control behaviour by drugs, which in some cases have been helpful. A great deal of research is being done that may benefit the mentally ill. The danger is that the same drugs in the hands of a world dictator could control an entire population of normal people. Stories from prisoners in oppressed countries verify how present-day mind manipulators misuse drugs to influence human actions.

One of them wrote: "I personally witnessed the treatment undergone by political prisoners in psychiatric hospitals when they tried to protest by refusing the food and the 'treatments' inflicted upon them. They were tied up, injected with paralysing sulphur and force fed... [They] have invented a powerful means to get rid of those who do not think as they do. Not only do they not hesitate to confine them in hospital-prisons, but they also compound their crime by injecting prisoners with chemical substances in order to destroy their personality and intellect."[4]

Changes in our body chemistry may benefit us or damage us

permanently. The determining question is, "Who administers the drugs and for what purpose?"

Experiments are being made to try to give one person the intellectual capacities of another by what the mind-manipulators call "artificial reincarnation." In a study that came out of Russia, it was reported that one of the country's top physicists had experimented with "tuning one mind to another telepathically." The scientist explained, " 'When this happens, the teacher can teach a student beyond the normal capacity of his mind by broadcasting over the defence mechanism into the normally empty 90 per cent of the brain.' " He continues to explain that he "reincarnated a European mathematical genius in a college maths student."[5]

Another human attempt to solve man's problems concerns *microbiology*. The increasing success with organ transplants may in time lead to a vast movement to change people by replacing certain organs connected with thinking, conscience, and emotions. However, the gospel of microbiology, administered by scientists who themselves are sinners, and who have access only to the substance of a fallen world, must likewise fail.

Many writers of science fiction consider their *interplanetary speculations* as the only source for solving man's problems. But the fundamental difficulty is that sin is too deeply ingrained in human nature to be rooted out by such influences. When God is ignored, the problem-solvers themselves participate in the problems. The superpowers are now frantically preparing for a "space" war. As a newspaper editorial says, "Whoever wins this race could control the world."

Many people today are trying to find a solution to man's problems by turning to *the occult world*. They seek knowledge and power from sources the Bible says we should wholeheartedly resist. The Apostle Paul says, "For our struggle is not against flesh and blood, but against the rulers, against the powers, against the world-forces of this darkness, against the spiritual forces of wickedness in the heavenly places" (Eph. 6:12). The occult world is a source only of terror and destruction.

The methods men use to change themselves from the outside in are truly varied, and sometimes amazing.

FROM THE INSIDE OUT

Jesus said that God can change men and women from the inside out. It was a challenge—a command. He didn't say, "It might be nice if you were born again," or, "If it looks good to you you might be born again." Jesus said, "You *must be* born again" (John 3:7).

It has always astounded me that He made this statement to a devout religious leader, Nicodemus, who must have been shocked by it. After all, Nicodemus was a good, moral, religious man. His neighbours probably said of him, "He's a wonderful man. You could trust him with your life. He's a great theologian." Nicodemus fasted two days a week; he spent two hours a day in prayer at the temple and tithed all his income. He was a professor of theology at the local seminary. If a pastor-seeking committee were looking for the best man they could get for their local church, they would seek a man like Nicodemus. But Jesus said all his piety and goodness weren't enough. He said, "You must be born again."

In spite of all of his education and professional standing, Nicodemus saw something very special in Jesus Christ—something he couldn't understand. He saw in Jesus a new quality of living. He was honestly seeking to find out what this dimension of life was.

When Jesus told him that unless one is born again he cannot see the kingdom of God, He was explaining to Nicodemus that he didn't have to improve his moral standards or increase his educational credits, he needed to receive a new quality of life—eternal life—that begins in this world and carries into the next world.

On returning home from a trip one day I found my desk, as usual, piled high with letters to be answered. In this particular pile there happened to be two from two separate mental hospitals in different states. A glance at the handwriting and a reading of the letters made it clear that the writers needed to be in a mental institution. Yet each spoke of the Lord Jesus and the comfort He was.

I could not help thinking how kind and understanding and compassionate God has been in choosing to reveal Himself to man through simple childlike faith rather than the intellect. There would otherwise be no chance for little children or the mentally retarded or brain damaged. And yet the brilliant scientist, the true intellectual, the genius, must all come the same way. As Jesus said in Matthew 18:3, "Unless you are converted and become like children, you shall not enter the kingdom of heaven."

John Hunter, the English Bible scholar, tells the story about a young man who came up to him after he had been preaching on John 3. "He, like Nicodemus, was obviously very well educated, and he said: 'What you have been saying has really challenged me; in fact, if I could fully understand what you have told us, I would become a real Christian.' He was quite sincere in what he said, so I questioned him and talked further with him. He was a graduate of a university, trained to think and evaluate facts.

"I asked, 'If you could really understand the full meaning of the gospel, you would become a Christian?'

" 'Yes,' he replied, 'I would.'

" 'Well, consider this,' I went on. 'I have a friend who is a missionary in the Congo. He works among the Pygmies, people with little capacity for understanding. If, in order to become a Christian, we had to understand the gospel message, how could these simple people ever be blessed?'

"His reply was quite honest: 'You know, I never thought of that?'

" 'No,' I replied, 'but God did. The gospel message doesn't have to be understood by the seeking soul, only to be received in simple faith. It isn't fully understanding the gospel that gives me the blessing, but simply believing and receiving it.'

"Nicodemus began by 'knowing,' but he continued by

believing and receiving."[6]

There are many people sitting in churches today who have never heard this message of the new birth. Some churches preach good works, social change, government legislation, and neglect the one thing that will help solve the problems of our world—changed men and women. Man's basic problem is first spiritual, then social. He needs a complete change from inside out.

Some time ago I attended a historic conference in Africa. Every country except one from the whole continent of Africa was represented by delegates. Never before had there been such a Christian gathering. Time after time I heard African leaders express appreciation for what Christian missions had done, especially in the fields of evangelism, medical aid, and education. One of the speakers said, "85 percent of all education south of the Sahara has been done by Christian missions."

An Anglican bishop from England told us, "Every social agency in England from the Royal Society for the Prevention of Cruelty to Animals, on up, was founded as a result of a conversion to Christ and a spiritual awakening." We must be careful not to put the cart before the horse.

The Bible refers many times to this change Jesus talked about. Through the prophet Ezekiel, God said, "I will give you a new heart and put a new spirit within you" (Ezek. 36:26). In the book of Acts, Peter called it repenting and being converted. Paul speaks of it in Romans as being "alive from the dead" (Rom. 6:13). In Colossians Paul calls it "[a putting off of] the old self with its evil practices, and [a putting on of] the new self who is being renewed to a true knowledge according to the image of the One who created him" (Col. 3:9,10). In Titus he calls it "the washing of regeneration and renewing by the Holy Spirit" (Tit. 3:5). Peter said it was being "partakers of the divine nature" (2 Pet. 1:4). In the Church of England catechism it is called "a death unto sin and a new birth unto righteousness."

The context of John 3 teaches that the new birth is something that God does for man when man is willing to yield to God. We have seen that the Bible teaches that man is dead in trespasses and sins, and his great need is life. We do not have within ourselves the seed of the new life; this must come from God Himself.

One of the great Christian writers of this century, Oswald Chambers, said, "Our part as workers for God is to open men's eyes that they may turn themselves from darkness to light; but that is not salvation, that is conversion—the effort of a roused human being. I do not think it is too sweeping to say that the majority of nominal Christians are of this order; their eyes are opened, but they have received nothing. ... When a man is born again, he knows that it is because he has received something as a gift from Almighty God and not because of his own decision."[7]

Conversion means "turning." The Bible is full of this concept and God pleads with man to turn to Him. He spoke through the prophet Ezekiel, "Repent ... and *turn* your faces away from all your abominations" (Ezek. 14:6, emphasis mine). Another prophet, Isaiah, spoke, "*Turn* to Me, and be saved, all the ends of the earth; for I am God, and there is no other" (Isa. 45:22, emphasis mine).

The new birth is not just being reformed, it's being transformed. People are always making resolutions to do better, to change, and breaking those resolutions soon afterwards. But the Bible teaches us that through the new birth we can enter a new world.

The contrasts used in the Bible to express the change which comes over us when we are born again are very graphic: from lust to holiness; from darkness to light; from death to resurrection; from stranger to the kingdom of God to now being its citizen. The Bible teaches that the person who is born again has a changed will, changed affections, changed objectives for living, changed disposition, new purpose. He receives a new nature and a new heart. He becomes a new creation.

BEFORE AND AFTER

The Bible is full of people from all walks of life who have been changed by an encounter with Jesus Christ. Christ met a woman in Samaria who was a prostitute and an outcast in her own town. To avoid meeting other women she went to a well during the heat of the day when she knew she wouldn't encounter other villagers. But there she met Christ. She was changed immediately into a new person. In fact, she became an instant missionary and rushed to her own city, where she was despised and scorned, to tell others about Jesus Christ. And we are told, "Many of the Samaritans believed in Him because of the word of the woman who testified, 'He told me all the things that I have done' " (John 4:39).

Andrew was an ordinary fellow. He didn't seem to be the big personality man, but he was very quick to respond to Christ; in fact, he was on fire from the moment he met Jesus. The first thing he did was to go and find his brother to tell him the wonderful news about the Messiah. He may not have been a flaming evangelist, but wherever he appears in the biblical account, he is fruitful.

In these days of high taxes, the yearly or quarterly tax reports are not exactly greeted with enthusiasm. It wasn't any different in Jesus' time. Zacchaeus, a tax collector, and not a very honest one at that, was skilful in defrauding people, but when he met Jesus all that changed. He repented and wanted to make amends for his deceitful acts. "Behold, Lord, half of my possessions I will give to the poor, and if I have defrauded anyone of anything, I will give back four times as much" (Luke 19:8).

A young intellectual named Saul was on a journey along the road to Damascus, persecuting Christians, when he met Jesus Christ. To this day we speak about "Damascus Road experiences," because Saul was never the same again. He became the great Apostle Paul. Many times he referred to that encounter, even recalling the very day and moment when he met Christ.

On the day of Pentecost a dramatic change occurred in three thousand people who were born again. In the morning they were lost, uncertain about the purpose of life, many of them guilty over the death of Christ. Others were afraid of either the secular or religious authorities. But at the end of the day they had been born into the kingdom of God. Each one had passed out of death into life. " 'Truly, truly, I say to you, he who hears My word, and believes Him who sent Me, has eternal life, and does not come into judgment, but has passed out of death into life' " (John 5:24).

Any person who is willing to trust Jesus Christ as his personal Saviour and Lord can receive the new birth now. It's not something to be received at death or after death; it is for now. "Now is the accepted time; behold, now is the day of salvation" (2 Cor. 6:2, AV).

THE NEW BIRTH IS FOR NOW

The "before and after" advertisements for diet remedies or face-lifts cannot match the impact of the testimonies of those who have been born again. From corporate president to prison inmate, stories unfold of lives turned right side up.

A young woman wrote us: "Until last January I was a stranger to Jesus. I was a rebel, thief, a drunkard, a hard drug taker, an adulteress, a hippie, and a self-centred, confused young woman. Thinking I was going to stump everyone with my cynical questions, I went to a Bible study about a year ago out of curiosity. That night I became sincerely interested in the Bible. Finally after searching and studying the Scriptures for months, John 3:16 spoke to my heart and I gave my life to Christ. I never knew that this kind of happiness could exist. God shows you how to love and what it feels like to be loved. He was what I had been looking for since my early teens. He was 'the bag' I hadn't found. It seemed to me that drugs, liquor, free love, and bumming around the country would make me free, but they were all traps. Sin was the trap that led me to confusion, unhappiness, guilt, and near-suicide. Christ has made me free. Being a Christian is exciting because there is always a new challenge, so much to learn. Now I wake up glad to see the day.

"He has made me new."

Johnny Cash says, "A few years ago I was hooked on drugs. I dreaded to wake up in the morning. There was no joy, peace, or happiness in my life. Then one day in my helplessness I turned my life completely over to God. Now I can't wait to get up in the morning to study my Bible. Sometimes the words out of the Scriptures leap into my heart. This does not mean that all my problems have been solved, or that I have reached any state of perfection. However, my life has been turned around. I have been born again!"

12

The New Birth Is Not Just a "Feeling"

A MAN WHO was persuaded to go to a large evangelistic meeting recalled the following events:

"It was here, I believe for the first time in my life, that I heard the claims of Jesus Christ presented, simply and authoritatively.

"At the end of his talk the speaker invited those who wished to know more to come to the front of the auditorium. I went and was introduced to the speaker and we talked for a while. There were other people who wanted to ask questions, so I made my way to the exit, very interested in what he had said, but still in a deep fog.

"Just as I was about to go out the door I was confronted by a man who looked me in the eye and said:

" 'Are you a Christian?'

" 'Strange question,' I thought, putting on my best Sunday school smile and saying, 'Oh yes, I think so.'

" 'Are you a Christian?' he insisted, a light in his eye.

" 'Crank,' I thought, 'Humour him and then escape!'

"So I replied, 'Well, I'm trying to be.'

" 'Ever try to be an elephant?'

"Grinning at my dumb astonishment, he took me by the arm, sat me down in a chair and explained that no amount of trying could ever transform me into a Christian (any more than it could turn me into an elephant). Then he began to explain what New Testament Christianity was all about. That Jesus Christ had died in *my* place. That He had paid the full penalty which *my* sins demanded. As I was, I stood condemned before a holy God; I needed a Saviour. Jesus alone could save me. Forgiveness for the past was possible in Him. Moreover, in His resurrection, He was offering me power to live the sort of life I had hitherto considered hopelessly out of reach.

"What a stupendous offer! If the living God were really asking to come into my wretched, tarnished life, to take over what I was only wasting and spoiling—how dare I refuse Him! He was promising, 'Behold, I stand at the door and knock.'

"I flung open the door. He was as good as His word."

This man was born again. He had a turnabout. He thought he was a Christian, but he had never personally made a commitment to Jesus Christ.

Jesus made everything so simple and we have made it so complicated. He spoke to the people in short sentences and everyday words, illustrating His messages with parables and stories.

Paul told the Philippian jailer who asked what he must do to be saved, "Believe in the Lord Jesus, and you shall be saved" (Acts 16:31).

It's so simple that it's often overlooked. Although the gospel message is heard—especially in America—on radio stations, presented on television, sung on street corners, presented from pulpits, and explained in books and tracts, millions overlook it.

All you have to do to be born again is to repent of your sins and believe in the Lord Jesus as your personal Lord and Saviour. You don't clean up, give up, or turn around yourself, you just come as you are. This is why we sing the hymn "Just As I Am" at our Crusades.

KEY WORD: REPENTANCE

In the New Testament Peter says, "Repent, therefore, and be *converted*, that your sins may be blotted out, [so that] the times of refreshing shall come from the presence of the Lord" (Acts 3:19, AV, emphasis mine).

A person cannot turn to God to repent, or even to believe, without God's help. God must do the turning. Many times the Bible tells how men and women did that very thing: "Turn thou me, and I shall be turned; for thou art the Lord my God" (Jer. 31:18, AV).

To many the word "repentance" is old-fashioned. It doesn't seem to have a proper place in a twentieth-century vocabulary. But repentance is one of the two vital elements in conversion and simply means recognition of what we are, and a willingness to change our minds toward sin, self, and God.

Repentance involves first of all an acknowledgment of our sin. When we repent we are saying that we recognise that we are sinners and that our sin involves us in personal guilt before God. This type of guilt does not mean incriminating self-contempt; it means seeing ourselves as God sees us, and saying, "God be merciful to me a sinner" (Luke 18:13, AV). It is not just the corporate guilt of society we are acknowledging—it's so easy to blame the government, the school system, the church, the home, for our own personal guilt. The Bible teaches that when we reach the age of accountability—usually somewhere around ten or eleven years of age—God looks upon us as full-grown adults, making moral and spiritual choices for which we will be held accountable at the judgment. Each of us has an individual guilt before God. From the moment we are conceived we have the tendency toward sin; then we become sinners by choice and, ultimately, sinners by practice. That is why the Bible says we have all sinned and come short of the glory of God.

Every person throughout the world, of whatever race, colour, language, or culture, needs to be born again. We are guilty of "sin" (singular) which is expressed in "sins" (plural). We break God's law and rebel against Him because we are sinners by nature. It is this disease of sin (singular) that Christ dealt with on the cross.

We have heard so much about "roots." The roots of man's individual and corporate problems lie deep in his own heart. We are a diseased human race. This disease can only be dealt with by the blood of Christ, just as in the Old Testament blood was shed on hundreds of altars, looking forward to the day when Jesus Christ would come and be "the Lamb of God who takes away the sin of the world" (John 1:29). He became the cosmic scapegoat for the entire world. All of our sins were laid on Him. This is why God can now forgive us. This is why He can infuse new life into us—which is called regeneration, or the new birth.

When we look at the attributes of God and realise how far short we fall of His perfection, there is no alternative to the recognition of our sinful nature. The Apostle Peter had been involved in sinful acts and harboured sinful thoughts, but far deeper than the physical or mental admission of wrongdoing, Peter realised that he had a twisted nature. He said, "Depart from me, for I am a sinful man, O Lord!" (Luke 5:8). Notice that he didn't say, "I sin," but "I am a sinful man."

Job saw how corrupt he was in relation to God's perfection, and said,"I have heard of Thee by the hearing of the ear; but now mine eye seeth Thee: Wherefore I abhor myself, and repent in dust and ashes" (Job 42:5,6, AV). Job compared himself with God and repented; he recognised what he was before God.

Repentance also involves a genuine *sorrow* for sin. Sorrow is an emotion, and we are creatures who vary greatly in the degree of sorrow we may experience. Repentance without sorrow is hollow, however. The Apostle Paul said, "I now rejoice, not that you were made sorrowful, but that you were made sorrowful to the point of repentance; for you were made sorrowful according to the will of God, in order that you might not suffer loss in anything through us" (2 Cor. 7:9).

With repentance comes a change of purpose, a willing turnaround from sin. If we had to repent without God's help, then we would be almost helpless. The Scripture teaches that we are dead in trespasses and in sins. A dead man can do nothing; therefore we need God's help even in our repenting. Sometimes this involves "restitution." If we have stolen, lied, or cheated to the hurt of other people, we must go and make this right if at all possible.

I've had hundreds of letters from people who have told me that they have had money returned to them that had been stolen by people who claimed to be "born again." Many people, before their conversion, have been shoplifters. Many have felt that they must go back to the store, discuss their wrongdoing with the manager, and make restitution.

When my wife was counselling with Joe Medina after he was tempted and helped a friend rob a filling station, she told him that his repentance would never be real unless he confessed his crime. He did. He earned the money that summer and returned it in full. The filling station owner forgave him. Today that young man has finished four years at a Bible college and is now a minister.

When Jim Vaus, the underworld figure, came to Christ in 1949, he spent many weeks looking up people whom he had offended, injured, and stolen from. He returned everything he possibly could and apologised to all those whom he had offended.

This type of restitution is rare today, but it is most certainly taught in the Scriptures. It helps complete our repentance. It shows to those whom we have offended, and to the world, that we mean business with God.

When emotions are contrary to our willingness to turn from

sin, hypocrisy enters the life of a believer, and doubts begin to grow. There are so many things in the Bible that seem so difficult to believe. When we become a new creature in Christ, we are propelled into an exhilarating, joyful, exciting experience which carries us emotionally for a time. Then doubts may enter our lives, quietly at first, but then more boldly as the questions begin to crowd out the trust. "How can I be willing to turn over my life to God when He might make me do something I don't want to do?"

When a wealthy, beautiful woman who was a leader in her community was converted, one of the first persons she told, a friend of many years, said, "Well, Dorothy, what are you going to do now—go to Africa as a missionary?"

Dorothy struggled with her emotions, but answered with her surrendered will, "If that's where God wants me, I'll go."

But it's not that easy for most to be willing to turn over the action and direction to God.

A wonderful old woman who wrote one of the classics in Christian books told a story about a young man of great intelligence who was having tremendous difficulties in his new Christian experience with this matter of will. He was a great doubter, and emotionally nothing seemed real to him. He was given this piece of advice: " 'A man's will is really the man's self; … what his will does, he does. Your part then is simply to put your will … over on God's side, making up your mind that you will believe what He says [in the Bible], because He says it, and that you will not pay any regard to the feelings that make it seem so unreal. God will not fail to respond, sooner or later, with His revelation to such a faith.'

"The young man paused a moment, and then said solemnly, 'I understand, and will do what you say. I cannot control my emotions, but I can control my will; and the new life begins to look possible to me, if it is only my will that needs to be set straight in the matter. I can give my will to God, and I do.' "[1]

Biblical repentance is the fuel which is used to propel our life

with God at the controls. Until we utilise that fuel, we are
earthbound, tied down by our ego, our pride, our troubles and
guilt. Young people are often chained in a prison of
purposelessness, uncertainty, and even guilt. Many an older
person faces old age and death with dread and fear. True
repentance can release those chains.

Thus, repentance is *first*, and absolutely necessary, if we are to
be born again. It involves simple recognition of what we are
before God—sinners who fall short of His glory; *second*, it
involves genuine sorrow for sin; *third*, it means our willingness
to turn from sin.

KEY WORD: FAITH

In considering conversion we have seen that it has a "turning-
from" side called repentance. It also has a "turning-to" side,
called faith.

Faith is first of all belief—belief that Christ was who He said
He was. Second, faith is belief that He can do what He claimed He
could do—He can forgive me, and come into my life. Third, faith
is trust, an act of commitment, in which I open the door of my
heart to Him. In the New Testament the words "faith," "belief,"
and "believe" are translations of similar Greek words so they are
interchangeable.

Placing your faith in Christ means that first you must make a
choice. The Scripture says, "Whoever believes in Him [Jesus] is
not condemned, but whoever does not believe stands condemned
already because he has not believed in the name of God's one and
only Son" (John 3:18, NIV). The person who believes is not
condemned; the person who has not believed is condemned. In
order not to be condemned you must make a choice—you must
choose to believe.

So we can see how important belief is. The Bible says that
without faith it is impossible to please God. But what does it mean
to believe? It means to "commit" yourself to Christ, to

"surrender" to Him. Believing is your response to God's offer of mercy, love, and forgiveness. God took the initiative and did everything that was needed to make the offer of salvation possible. When Christ bowed His head on the cross and said, "It is finished," He meant just that (John 19:30). God's plan for our reconciliation and redemption was complete in His Son. But only by believing in Jesus—committing yourself to Him, surrendering to Him—are you saved.

Belief is not just a feeling; it is the assurance of salvation. You may look at yourself in the mirror and say, "But I don't feel saved—I don't feel forgiven." But don't depend on feelings for your assurance. Christ has promised, and He cannot lie. Belief is a deliberate act of committing one's self to the person of Jesus Christ. It's not a "hanging on" to some vague idea. It is an act of trust in the God-Man, Jesus Christ.

The New Testament never used the words "belief" and "faith" in the plural. Christian faith does not mean accepting a long list of dos and don'ts. It means a single, individual relinquishment of mind and heart toward the one person, Jesus Christ. It does not mean believing everything or just anything. It is belief in a person, and that person is the Christ described in Scripture.

Faith is not anti-intellectual. Faith involves a very logical premise—that is, trusting that God's superior ability is able to save us.

Francis Schaeffer, a brilliant Christian living in Switzerland, explains that faith is not only logical, but that lack of faith is illogical. He writes: "Man is made in the image of God; therefore, on the side of the fact that God is a personal God the chasm stands not between God and man, but between man and all else. But on the side of God's infinity, man is as separated from God as the atom or any other finite [object] of the universe. So we have the answer to man's being finite and yet personal.

"It is not that this is the best answer to existence; it is the *only* answer. That is why we may hold our Christianity with intellectual integrity. The only answer for what exists is that He, the infinite-personal God, really is there."[2]

Faith in Christ is also voluntary. A person cannot be coerced, bribed, or tricked into trusting Jesus. God will not force His way into your life. The Holy Spirit will do everything possible to disturb you, draw you, love you—but finally it is your personal decision. God not only gave His Son on the cross where the plan of redemption was finished: He gave the law as expressed in the Ten Commandments and the Sermon on the Mount to show you your need of forgiveness; He gave the Holy Spirit to convict you of your need. He gives the Holy Spirit to draw you to the cross, but even after all of this, it is your decision whether to accept God's free pardon or to continue in your lost condition.

Faith also involves the whole person. In his book *Knowing God*, J. I. Packer says, "Knowing God is a matter of *personal involvement*, in mind, will, and feeling. It would not, indeed, be a fully personal relationship otherwise."[3]

So faith is not just an emotional reaction, an intellectual realisation, or a wilful decision; faith is all-inclusive. It involves the intellect, the emotion, and the will.

STEPS LEADING TO CONVERSION

We have seen that conversion occurs when we repent and place our faith in Christ. But what is the process like as we approach the point of conversion? How long will it take? Will it be emotional or dramatic? My answer is, I don't know. If everyone had the same reaction we could apply a neat little chemical formula with predetermined results. The key word is *variety*.

We can see this clearly if we stop for a moment to reflect on God. First, the point we are heading for is a point where God Himself is going to do something; He is the one who converts us when we repent and believe in Christ. "Salvation is of the Lord." Second, His help starts coming long before that point. As we have already seen, during the time before conversion He is preparing us for repentance by the conviction of the Holy Spirit and by making us want to turn from our sins. Also He is preparing us for faith by showing us how forgiving and majestic Christ is.

Questions about length of time and amount of emotion in the conversion process, consequently, are very personal. God looks at each of us differently, because each of us is different. He will relate to you just as you are. He will relate to me just as I am. Of course, in His concern His goal for each of us will be the same— our new birth. But to help us to that point He will be just as personal as a shepherd who knows each of his sheep by name.

We could go to the experiences of people we know, or to your own experience. If you have not been born again, the very fact that you are reading this book right now may be the process God is using in your life to lead you toward a decision.

God knows the needs of your heart. When we look at the process He used with different people in the Bible prior to their conversion, we see that He understands their individuality. In John 1, for instance, He talked to several men who had not yet been converted. On being approached by Andrew and a friend, Jesus asked a question, "What do you seek?" (John 1:38), and then invited them to spend the day with Him where He was staying. Quiet conversation was Andrew's need if he was to gain a sense of his sin and a trust in Jesus.

Andrew brought along his erratic brother, Simon. Christ acted very differently toward him. Regarding him seriously, Jesus said, "You are Simon the son of John; you shall be called 'Cephas' (which translated means Peter)," the word for rock. Jesus revealed a flash of His majesty by telling this volatile young man that in trusting Him his character would be changed to a rocklike steadiness (John 1:42). To be converted Peter needed to see his sin of relying on himself, which made him such a changeable personality, and he needed to trust Christ as the One who had the power and concern to change him.

The next day Jesus found Philip and treated him in still another way. He simply said, "Follow Me" (John 1:43). Unlike Andrew or Peter, Philip needed a straightforward command. Philip then brought Nathanael, a very religious man of prayer who was seeking an experience with God. Jesus adapted to his special needs in John 1:51, saying, "Truly, truly, I say to you, you shall see the heavens opened, and the angels of God ascending and descending upon the Son of Man."

Andrew, Peter, Philip, and Nathanael were all different. So Jesus treated them all differently. They all needed a personal relationship with Christ. This is essentially what the new birth is. To some of them the realisation of what was happening came slowly. It took months of training by Jesus Himself. This is why I urge new converts to take plenty of time in Bible study and prayer before getting on a public platform to testify. The Scripture warns against "a novice." We have often unwittingly been guilty of this in our Crusades—putting up to give a testimony young converts who had really not grown in the grace and knowledge of Christ enough. Through long years of experience we have become far more careful.

After his conversion, the Apostle Paul took three years of study in Arabia. It took God forty years to train Moses on the back side of a desert before he made his public appearance. In these days we often hear of a person who is in jail one day, and a few weeks later is on a public platform testifying concerning his conversion before a large crowd. Sometimes this is followed by a great tragedy—the so-called new convert had really not been born again; he had only professed Christ but had not been willing to pay the price of following Christ.

I know a young man who seemed to be gloriously converted in one of our Crusades, and I believe he was. He did have a rather long period of getting over his drug habit and growing in the knowledge of the Scriptures. We urged him to attend a Bible school, which he did for a year. His testimony was so thrilling that the invitations began to pour in from across America for him to give his witness. It wasn't long before this attention had caused him to backslide terribly, to the point of even leaving his wife and family. I am glad to report that he has been restored to fellowship with God, realises his sins and mistakes, and is now going back to finish his studies.

What can we expect the process to be like as we approach the new birth? It will be tailored to our own environment, temperament, secret needs, and hopes. That is the way God works.

HOW LONG ARE THE STEPS?

The length of time and degree of emotion involved in the process which leads to our conversion are also varied. Some, but not all, will face an emotional crisis with symptoms similar to those accompanying mental conflict. They may experience deep feelings and even tears of repentance. The Holy Spirit is convicting them of sin. This is their way of responding to Him. Each of us may have a different emotional experience. The night I came to Christ there were several people around me weeping. I had no tears at all and wondered if my act of commitment was genuine.

I have learned since that many have had a much quieter conversion, with a shorter time in the process. Perhaps one person, reading the Scripture or singing a hymn, comes upon a simple statement and applies it to himself then and there. Another person hears a sermon and with no stress or conflict receives its message and believes in Christ. Conversion is no less real to these quiet people than to the more expressive or dramatic ones.

Acts 16 records two conversions which were striking contrasts. Lydia was a businesswoman in the city of Philippi. She had shown enough interest in God to be spending time and prayer by the side of a river, where she heard Paul preach. The Lord opened her heart to respond to the gospel message, and she was converted without fanfare or a strong emotional display.

Then there was the jailer in the city of Philippi where Paul was imprisoned. An earthquake came and the jailer panicked as he realised his prisoners could escape. He thought the only way out of his crisis was to kill himself. Just as he was drawing his sword he heard the Apostle Paul say, "Do yourself no harm, for we are all here!" (Acts 16:28).

The jailer couldn't believe what he heard! Why hadn't the prisoners escaped? He was shaking from head to foot, and called for a light. He took one look at Paul and Silas, his prisoners, and fell down at their feet, crying, "What must I do to be saved?" Paul told him to believe in the Lord Jesus Christ and he would be saved, and he was converted right there, in the rubble of the prison.

Jesus described the conversion experience like the movement of the wind. "The wind blows where it wishes and you hear the sound of it, but do not know where it comes from and where it is going; so is every one who is born of the Spirit" (John 3:8).

Wind can be quiet, gentle, or it can reach cyclone proportions. So it is with conversion, sometimes easy and tender, and other times a tornado which alters the entire landscape.

Is there one definite point in time, one hour of one day of one year when a person can say, "That was when I was born again"? I know many people who can point to that time and say with assurance, "That was my spiritual birthday." However, I know there are people who today are walking in fellowship with Jesus Christ, but have no memory of an exact time when they deliberately committed themselves to Him, and cannot remember when they did not love and trust Him. My wife is one of those great Christians in this category. However, it is my opinion that they may be the exception rather than the rule. Scripture teaches that belief is an act of the will, so whether they can remember the time or not, there was a moment when they crossed over the line from death to life.

Nevertheless, the issue for a person now is not so much "when" as "whether." When we were saved is not so important as whether we are now saved. We often cannot tell the exact moment when night becomes day, but we know when it is daylight. So the great question for a person to answer who has never by a conscious act of will committed himself to Christ as his Lord and Saviour is this: "Are you now living in the day, in touch with Christ?"

HOW TO RECEIVE CHRIST

Just after I received Christ someone gave me a little tract entitled "Four Things God Wants You To Know," by an English writer. I often used those four points in my earlier preaching, and they were excellent. Years later, Bill Bright of Campus Crusade developed "The Four Spiritual Laws" which have been widely used throughout the world in helping people to understand how to be born again. Our own organisation developed what we called "Four Steps to Peace with God," taken largely from one of my earlier books, *Peace with God*. I do not believe, however, that there is a tidy little formula, or a recipe which has the Good Housekeeping seal of approval. However, I do believe these have provided little handles which help people to understand how to receive Christ.

Here are some guidelines from the Bible which will help you accept Christ as your Lord and Saviour. You have seen the need, the direction, and the steps in previous chapters, and you may already have reached your own conclusions. Just the same, let me summarise what you must do.

First, you must recognise what God did: that He loved you so much He gave His Son to die on the cross. Substitute your own name for "the world" and "whoever" in this familiar verse: "For God so loved the world, that He gave His only begotten Son, that whoever believes in Him should not perish, but have eternal life" (John 3:16). "The Son of God ... loved me, and delivered Himself up for me" (Gal. 2:20).

Second, you must repent for your sins. Jesus said, "Unless you repent, you will ... perish" (Luke 13:3). He said "Repent and believe" (Mark 1:15). It's not enough to be sorry; repentance is that turnabout from sin that is emphasised.

Third, you must receive Jesus Christ as Saviour and Lord. "But as many as received Him, to them He gave the right to become children of God, even to those that believe in His name" (John 1:12). This means that you cease trying to save yourself and accept Christ as your only Lord and your only Saviour. Trust Him completely, without reservation.

Fourth, you must confess Christ publicly. This confession is a sign that you have been converted. Jesus said, "Every one therefore who shall confess Me before men, I will also confess him before My Father who is in heaven" (Matt. 10:32). It is extremely important that when you receive Christ you tell someone else about it just as soon as possible. This gives you strength and courage to witness.

Make it happen *now*. "Now is the accepted time ... now is the day of salvation" (2 Cor. 6:2, AV). If you are willing to repent for your sins and to receive Jesus Christ as your Lord and Saviour, you can do it now. At this moment you can either bow your head or get on your knees and say this little prayer which I have used with thousands of persons on every continent:

O God, I acknowledge that I have sinned against You. I am sorry for my sins. I am willing to turn from my sins. I openly receive and acknowledge Jesus Christ as my Saviour. I confess Him as Lord. From this moment on I want to live for Him and serve Him. In Jesus' name. Amen.

These are the steps and the prayer which many years ago, in a book I wrote, were read by people just like yourselves who responded and wrote of their changed lives.

If you are willing to make this decision and have received Jesus Christ as your own Lord and Saviour, then you have become a child of God in whom Jesus Christ dwells. You do not need to measure the certainty of your salvation by your feelings. Believe God. He keeps His word. You are born again. You are alive!

(If you would like more help and literature, please feel free to write me:

Billy Graham
Minneapolis, Minnesota, U.S.A.

—that's all the address you need.)

13

Alive and Growing

"AFTER THINKING ABOUT it for three days, I realised I needed Jesus Christ, and I accepted Him. Now that my life has been turned over to Jesus Christ, I can function with an extra power bestowed by God."

Who made a statement like that? Someone down on the bottom of life's heap, struggling for worth and identity? No. A handsome, young University of Southern California athlete John Naber, who gained international attention by earning four gold medals with his swimming achievements in the 1976 Olympics. John Naber said he was searching for something meaningful in his life and after attending one of our meetings he began to wake up to the realisation of Jesus Christ. He was born again.

More and more celebrities, especially in the sports, entertainment, and political worlds, are telling of their new experiences of being made alive in Christ. While it is thrilling to hear about it, there are also dangers (as I have already expressed) in a "novice" who has very little grounding in the Word of God. Yet I cannot help rejoicing in every one of them and I believe that

God has been moving mightily in reaching out for people of extraordinary gifts and talents all over the world. Many of them He is greatly using to win others to Christ. A newspaper feature said that "evidence of a current religious revival is everywhere," and then related how famous personalities were "pinpointing the exact moment of spiritual turn-around" with their "often unbelievable accounts of being born again. Some say they have met Jesus Christ. Others experience a sensation similar to an electric shock. In all cases the new believers experience overwhelming feelings of love and joy."

Dean Jones, a Walt Disney film veteran, relates, "I was performing in summer stock at a New Jersey lodge and had gone to my room to be alone. Nothing was satisfying me. I looked out that window and felt fear and confusion. Impulsively, I knelt by the bed and spelled out my doubts to God; I don't know why I was moved to do this. I said to God, 'If you bring meaning to my life, I'll serve you.' "

There is nothing more exciting than a personal testimony from a person who has experienced a spiritual rebirth. This is more than an interesting story or fascinating experience. A newborn man or woman has been given so many riches by God. We will outline them and then discuss how to draw from that wealthy potential.

FORGIVEN!

"Your sins are forgiven you for His name's sake" (1 John 2-12). What a stupendous promise! Throughout the New Testament we learn that the one who receives Christ as Lord and Saviour also receives, immediately, the gift of forgiveness. The Bible says, "As far as the east is from the west, so far has He removed our transgressions from us" (ps. 103:12).

"Forgive me." "I'm sorry." "I didn't mean it." How often we use those words and they echo back with a hollow sound. But God's forgiveness is not just a casual statement; it is the complete blotting out of all the dirt and degradation of our past, present, and future. The only reason our sins can be forgiven is because Jesus Christ paid their full penalty on the cross.

Guilt feelings provide the basis for many dramatic plots. Shakespeare's line from *Macbeth* is famous: "Out, damned spot! Out!" Guilt feelings are the focal point of much psychiatric counselling. Many feel like Judas, who, after he betrayed Christ, said, "I have betrayed innocent blood." So tremendous is the weight of our guilt that the great and glorious concept of forgiveness should be shouted by every believer in Jesus Christ.

God's goodness in forgiving us goes even farther when we realise that when we are converted we are also declared just—which means that in God's sight we are without guilt, clothed forever with Christ's righteousness.

As we saw in "The King's Courtroom," forgiveness and justification are God's free gifts.

ADOPTED BY THE KING

When you were converted, God adopted you as His son or daughter. As an adopted child each of us can claim to be a joint heir with Jesus Christ. "God sent forth His Son ... that He might redeem those who were under the Law, that we might receive the adoption as sons" (Gal. 4:4,5).

I know a lawyer and his wife who have two adopted children, a boy and a girl. The little girl looks very much like her mother, and the young man could easily be the natural son of his father. The fact that they were chosen by their parents has given them a great sense of security and love.

To be the son or daughter of the Lord of the universe is a powerful realisation.

THE INDWELLING HOLY SPIRIT

When you were converted, the Spirit of God immediately came

to live in you. Before He ascended into heaven, Jesus Christ said, "I will ask the Father, and He will give you another Helper, that He may be with you forever; that is the Spirit of truth ... you know Him, because He abides with you, and will be in you" (John 14:16,17).

When Christ lived on this earth, He could be with only a small group of people at any one time. Now Christ dwells through the Holy Spirit in the hearts of all those who have received Him as Lord and Saviour. Lloyd Ogilvie, pastor of the First Presbyterian Church in Hollywood, refers to the Holy Spirit as "the contemporary Christ." Paul wrote to the Romans, "He [God] ... will also give life to your mortal bodies through His Spirit who indwells you" (Rom. 8:11).

At the historic Congress on World Evangelisation in Switzerland in 1974, the Holy Spirit was the subject of many addresses and discussions. The Reverend Gottfried Osei-Mensah of Nairobi, Kenya, said, "The Spirit is our Master. It is the work of the Holy Spirit, living in us, to free us from the rule of sin in our daily lives, and to help us live the new life we share with Christ."

How long does the Holy Spirit live in the heart of a believer? Forever. God does not give a gift as powerful as the Holy Spirit and then take it back. By faith you accept God's statements that you are indwelt by the Spirit of God, but you can watch Him at work, too. The Holy Spirit can rejuvenate a tired Christian, captivate an indifferent believer, and empower a dry church.

A clergyman from Buenos Aires, Argentina, said, "the Holy Spirit today is renewing the fruit of the Spirit—love, joy, peace. All those things are going to be the elements that show the world that we are His people."

The Holy Spirit is there to give you special power to work for Christ. He is there to give you strength in the moment of temptation.

Jesus promised that we would receive power from the Holy Spirit (Acts 1:8). Perhaps you have heard the story of the woodpecker who was pecking with his beak against the trunk of a tree. At that very moment, the lightning struck the tree, splitting it from top to bottom. When he'd recovered from the shock, the woodpecker flew away exclaiming, "I didn't know there was so much power in my beak!" I don't ask you, have you the Holy Spirit, but does the Holy Spirit have you?

VICTORY OVER TEMPTATION

The Bible teaches that the new believer in Jesus Christ—the converted person—is to "abhor what is evil" (Rom. 12:9). Here is another strong admonishment: "In reference to your former manner of life, you lay aside the old self, which is being corrupted in accordance with the lusts of deceit" (Eph. 4:22).

Now wait a minute. How are we supposed to be able to stop doing some of the sinful things we have done for years, or get rid of some of the negative, suspicious, hateful, greedy attitudes which are ingrained in our personality? "I just can't do it myself," you might say.

You're right. However, the capacity to resist sin and obey God comes from the Holy Spirit, who lives in every true believer. It's not up to us to struggle against temptation alone. God lives in our hearts to help us resist sin. It is His job to work, and our job to yield.

What about the old bugaboo of temptation? The Bible doesn't say we won't be tempted; that would be foolish. We know that we live in a world full of temptations, most of them tied up in very attractive packages and offered as something we must try or buy—just once! But the converted man or woman has the offer of victory over temptation. "No temptation has overtaken you but such as is common to man; and God is faithful, who will not allow you to be tempted beyond what you are able; but with the temptation will provide the way of escape also, that you may be able to endure it" (1 Cor. 10:13).

To be tempted is not a sin; as a believer in Jesus Christ you do not need to blame yourself for an increase in the temptations that surround you. The indwelling Holy Spirit gives us strength to resist temptation.

Temptation is very powerful and will become even more so after you have been born again. The Scriptures tell us that we are in a spiritual warfare and that our enemies have more power and skill to tempt us than we have ever encountered before. Here is where many new believers make a big mistake. They think that when they are converted they will become perfect right away, that they will live on a continual high. Then they find themselves being tempted, in conflict, and even at times yielding to temptation. The new believer takes a look at himself and doesn't like what he sees. He is filled with discouragement and frustration. This is normal. The devil tempts you and God tests you. Often they are two sides to the same coin—God allows the devil to tempt you, and He uses it as a test, or as an experience to help deepen your faith and let you see how fragile you really are if you depend on yourself. He wants you to depend totally and completely on Him.

An old allegory illustrates this well: "Satan called together a council of his servants to consult how they might make a good man sin. One evil spirit started up and said, 'I will make him sin.'—'How will you do it?' asked Satan. 'I will set before him the pleasures of sin,' was the reply; 'I will tell him of its delights, and the rich rewards it brings.'—'Ah,' said Satan, 'that will not do; he has tried it, and knows better than that.' Then another imp started up and said 'I will make him sin.'—'What will you do?' asked Satan. 'I will tell him of the pains and sorrows of virtue. I will show him that virtue has no delights, and brings no rewards.'—'Ah, no!' exclaimed Satan, 'that will not do at all; for he has tried it, and knows that "Wisdom's ways *are* ways of pleasantness, and all her paths are peace." '—'Well,' said another imp, starting up, 'I will undertake to make him sin.'—'And what will you do?' asked Satan, again. 'I will discourage his soul,' was the short reply. 'Ah, that will do!' cried Satan; 'that will do! We shall conquer him now.' "[1]

Spiritual conflict is at work in the heart of every believer. It is true that the Christian possesses a new nature, but the old sin nature is still there. It is now up to us, day by day, to yield to the new nature which Christ dominates.

There is the story of a housewife who found a mouse in her kitchen and took a broom to it. The mouse didn't waste its time contemplating either the housewife or the broom, but got busy looking for the hole. And so it is with us when we are caught by temptation. We don't spend time contemplating the temptation but get busy looking for a way out. The Scripture says, "God ... will not allow you to be tempted beyond what you are able; but with the temptation will provide the way of escape also" (1 Cor. 10:13).

When the Christian sins he is miserable. Sometimes he avoids other Christians, stops going to church, believes that he is misunderstood. However, every Christian has access to God through prayer and when he confesses his sin God restores fellowship with him. This is the difference between the believer and the unbeliever. The unbeliever makes sin a practice; the believer does not.

A word about how believers should treat a "fallen" brother: Some years ago we knew a young student recently converted from a life of drugs. Shortly after his conversion he agreed to turn informer for a narcotics agent in order to try and catch the pushers in that area. Fellow Christians warned him against doing this, but he had already committed himself and the inevitable happened. He blew his Christian witness when he had to pretend to be a drug-user himself in order to convince the pusher that he was for real, at one point having to take two shots of heroin. (Incidentally, the shots had an effect on him opposite to that before his conversion—instead of getting high he had violent withdrawals.) The Sunday before he left the school to return to his home, he stood up before the Sunday school class to tell them what had happened. The pusher had been caught, and although this young man had blown his Christian witness, he wanted the students to know that he was still a believer and a follower of the Lord. He stood up before the class, holding two fingers together to explain, "Me and Jesus are just like this." This gave the teacher an opportunity to talk to the students on how a brother should be treated when he has apparently fallen. During the time when he was trying to assist the narcotics agent, all the Christians on campus, thought he had backslidden and gave him the cold shoulder. Actually, when we see a brother fall (or one whom we think has fallen) we should, like the Good Samaritan, get down and help him up again and do what we can to encourage him, pray for him, and let him know that we love him and believe in him.

The believer hates sin and wants to abide by God's commands. Paul says believers "do not walk according to the flesh, but according to the Spirit" (Rom. 8:4). The Holy Spirit who indwells us convicts us in various ways. A believer will begin to realise that the dirty jokes which were once a part of his office repertoire are sticking in his throat. The cocktail parties which were once so interesting and funny have become dull and boring. Ruth and I have sometimes gone to cocktail parties in various parts of the world. Always we have taken a soft drink and tried to be a witness. The first convert of the New York Crusade was a direct result of my going to a cocktail party like this on board a ship coming from Japan in the early 1950s. Such occasions may afford a great opportunity for Christian witness. We have often had a whole group of people gather around us and ask spiritual questions. In this same way Jesus talked with publicans and sinners, and for a clear purpose. On the other hand, going to cocktail parties just to be one of the gang not only often becomes boring, but carries the painful risk of hearing someone swear and take the name of the Lord in vain.

The choices of a new believer are made from a new perspective. He may hand himself over to sin (and feel miserable in it) or give himself over to God. Paul's advice is excellent: "I urge you therefore, brethren, by the mercies of God, to present your bodies a living and holy sacrifice, acceptable to God, which is your spiritual service of worship. And do not be conformed to this world, but be transformed by the renewing of your mind, that you may prove what the will of God is, that which is good and acceptable and perfect" (Rom. 12:1,2).

The transformation by "renewing of your mind" may happen quickly and dramatically, as the addict who experiences instant withdrawal, or it may permeate into your lifestyle more gradually.

GROWING SLOWLY, ALMOST IMPERCEPTIBLY—BUT GROWING!

Many people grow into Christian maturity very rapidly; others much more slowly, almost imperceptibly. I once saw a picture on television of flowers growing, budding, and opening. This was done by slow-motion photography over a long period of time. If you had watched the same process with your naked eye in your garden it would have taken days. In the same way, we watch our lives from day to day and often get discouraged at the slow growth. But if you wait for a year or two and then look back over your life you will see how much you have grown. You've become kinder, more gracious, more loving. You love the Scriptures more. You love to pray more. You are a more faithful witness. You never will reach that point of full maturity in Christ until you see Him face to face in heaven.

Abrupt or gradual, the changes in a converted person are a part of his growth. He is not reborn full-grown; rather he is reborn with the energies of new life that will mature him as time passes. This growth is spiritual and moral. It's just like a baby learning to crawl, then toddle, then walk, then run. It takes time, study, patience, and discipline.

A person can attempt to imitate Christian growth by religious effort, but the result is like a plaster of Paris model of Michelangelo's David. It's phony and easily broken.

A Christian grows as the life of God exerts its new power from deep in the centre of his personality. The unconverted person cannot duplicate that life, no matter how religious he tries to act. He lacks the sources for growth because he has not been reborn.

A group of students at Harvard once tried to fool the famous professor of zoology Agassiz. They took parts from a number of different bugs and with great skill attached them together to make a creation they were sure would baffle their teacher. On the chosen day they brought it to him and asked that he identify it. As he inspected it with great care, the students grew more and more sure they had tricked this genius.

Finally, Professor Agassiz straightened up and said, "I have identified it." Scarcely able to control their amusement, they asked its name. Agassiz replied, "It is a humbug."

A person with genuine life from God will detect the counterfeit and think, "Humbug."

The new convert is a babe in Christ. A babe must be nourished in order to grow. He must be protected because he has been born into a world of many enemies. His primary battle will be with "the world," "the flesh," and "the devil." This is why he needs the encouragement of his family, Christian friends, and especially the Church. At the time of birth the child of God is born into great riches, and has a marvellous inheritance, but it takes some time to find out about all his wealth.

The most important thing in the beginning of new life is to be nourished and strengthened. Here are the important nutrients to use.

GET A BIBLE

If you have a Bible, fine. If the Scriptures are a whole new world to you, however, I would advise that you get one of the newer translations which may be easier for you to understand. It is important for you to begin reading the New Testament, and the Gospel of John is a good place to start.

Saturate yourself in the Word of God. Don't worry about understanding everything you read, because you won't. Pray before you read and ask the Holy Spirit to clarify what you are reading. The Scriptures are the greatest source of hope you will find in this hopeless world. "For whatever was written in earlier times was written for our instruction, that through perseverance and the encouragement of the Scriptures we might have hope" (Rom. 15:4).

Memorise portions of the Word of God. "Thy word have I hid in mine heart, that I might not sin against thee" (Ps. 119:11, AV). Try taking a Bible verse that speaks to your needs and typing it on a file card. Put it in your pocket or purse and refer to it frequently. Review it daily, and by the end of the week you will have a verse memorised.

Satan is the great discourager. He doesn't want you to read the Bible or memorise Scripture. In the past you may not have been attacked by Satan, but now you've done something which makes him very angry. You've left his camp and joined the army of God. You're a Christian soldier and Satan will unleash all of his secret weapons. From now on it's upstream all the way against the current of the evils of this world.

But you can overcome everything he hurls at you with the weapon God has provided—"the sword of the Spirit, which is the word of God" (Eph. 6:17). Not only is the Word of God a sword to be used in offence, but you also have a shield to be used in defence. You have "the shield of faith, wherewith ye shall be able to quench all the fiery darts of the wicked" (Eph. 6:16, AV).

When Christ was in the wilderness He was tempted by Satan, and every time He met temptation with Scripture, saying, "It is written" (Matt. 4).

Christ needed this mighty weapon, and so do we.

LEARN TO PRAY

There are complete books written about prayer, seminars held which deal in prayer, and hundreds of sermons on the power of prayer. The new believer is sometimes baffled by what and how to pray.

Jesus said, "Men ought always to pray" (Luke 18:1, AV). The Apostle Paul said, "Pray without ceasing" (1 Thess. 5:17).

A prayer does not have to be eloquent or contain the language and terms of a theologian. When you made your decision for Christ, you were given the privilege of addressing God as Father. You pray to Him as a child talking to his loving and gracious father. In the beginning you may not be fluent, but it's important to begin. My wife has a notebook she has kept of our children as they were beginning to talk with us. She treasures these first attempts, mistakes and all. She said, "I wouldn't take anything for that book."

When Paul said we should pray without "ceasing," he chose a term used in his day to describe a persistent cough. Off and on throughout our day we should be turning quickly to God to praise and thank Him, and to ask for His help. Prayers should be specific. God is interested in everything you do and nothing is too great or too insignificant to share with Him.

FIND CHRISTIAN FELLOWSHIP

God doesn't intend for you to live the Christian life alone. This is why He has brought other believers together to form fellowships. A church where the Bible is taught and believed is the first place a reborn man or woman must seek. I do not advise that just any church will do. Is the pastor teaching the Word of God or expounding his own or some other philosophy of living? You'll know. Does the church have Bible classes for all ages?

Without the fellowship of believers, a newly born Christian has a tendency to wither. The writer of the Book of Hebrews says, "Let us consider how to stimulate one another to love and good deeds, not forsaking our own assembling together, as is the habit of some but encouraging one another" (Heb. 10:24,25).

Perhaps there's a Bible class or prayer group in your community. It's exciting to find a whole new set of friends, people who are in various stages of their own Christian growth, to share with and strengthen your faith.

One of my daughters lives in a high middle-class neighbourhood. Some of the social leaders of the city are her neighbours. After a great deal of prayer she decided that she would go to her neighbours' houses and ask them if they would like to have a Bible study. She knocked on the door of house after house, and in almost every instance the women not only said "yes," but some of them burst into tears and said, "I've been waiting for someone to ask me to a Bible class so I could learn the Bible." Today, my daughter teaches a weekly Bible class of three hundred women, with many on the waiting list to get in. If there's not a Bible class in your community, perhaps you could start one. You will find your neighbours "hungrier" and "thirstier" than you had ever dreamed. They are just waiting for someone to take the initiative. At first it may be that only two or three of you will meet, read a passage in the Bible, discuss it, have prayer over a cup of coffee. There are tens of thousands of such Bible classes springing up throughout the world in homes, in offices, in professional football teams. Even the touring golf professionals have a weekly Bible class that attracts anywhere from ten to fifty of the golfers and their wives.

You are no longer alone. The fatherhood of God forms the true brotherhood of man, an ideal which the philosophers and moralists have sought from the beginning of time. This brotherhood erases barriers of language, cultural background, and race. One of the greatest joys a Christian experiences is that of meeting a fellow believer in an unexpected place. The waitress in the restaurant finds a common bond with her customer. The passenger on an airplane discovers that the stewardess is a believer. You are in a foreign country and immediately feel at home when you encounter another Christian. No lengthy introductions are necessary. You share the greatest bond on earth.

There is no fellowship on earth to compare with it.

At the beginning of this book I said that I believed the most important subject in the entire world is that of the new birth. It is the most important event which can happen to any man, woman, or child.

It is only when you are born again that you can experience all the riches God has in store for you. You are not just a living person, you are truly ALIVE!

Notes

Notes

Preface

1. *Time,* September 27, 1976, p. 86
2. *Los Angeles Times,* September 23, 1976, pp. 3, 30.
3. Corrie ten Boom, *In My Father's House* (London: Hodder & Stoughton, 1977)

Chapter One

1. Charles Colson, *Born Again* (London: Hodder & Stoughton, 1976)
2. Bertrand Russell, *Power: A New Social Analysis* (New York: Norton, 1938), p. 11.
3. H. R. Rookmaaker, *Modern Art and the Death of a Culture* (London: Inter-Varsity Press, 1970), p. 196.
4. Ibid., p. 202.
5. Os Guinness, *Dust of Death* (London: Inter-Varsity Press, 1973)
6. Hal Lindsey, *The Terminal Generation* (Old Tappan, N.J.: Fleming H. Revell Co., 1976), p. 83.
7. Rookmaaker, *Modern Art,* p. 223.
8. Guinness, *Dust of Death.*

Chapter Three

1. Josh McDowell, *Evidence That Demands a Verdict* (Campus Crusade for Christ, 1972), p. 17 ff.

Chapter Four

1. Sir James Frazer, *The Golden Bough* (London: Macmillan, 1936).
2. Ibid.,
3. Walter Kaufmann, *Critique of Religion and Philosophy* (New York: Harper and Row, 1958), p. 74.
4. Ibid., p. 88.
5. Tw. W. Doane, *Bible Myths* (New York: University Books, 1971), p. 252.
6. *Time*, December 30, 1974, p. 38.
7. Ibid., p. 40.

Chapter Five

1. *Time*, June 30, 1975, p. 10.
2. *Time*, February 2, 1976, p. 62.
3. William Barclay, *Letters to Timothy* (Philadelphia: Westminster Press, 1960), p. 44

Chapter Six

1. *Time*, February 7, 1977, p. 37

Chapter Seven

1. Josh McDowell, *Evidence That Demands a Verdict* (Campus Crusade, 1972), p. 89.

2. Harry Rimmer, *The Magnificence of Jesus* (Grand Rapids, Mich.: Wm. B. Eerdmans Publishing Co., 1943), p. 112.
3. C. S. Lewis, *Surprised by Joy* (London: Fontana Books, 1959).

Chapter Nine

1. Nicolaus von Zinzendorf, 1739, tr. John Wesley, 1940.
2. *Saturday Evening Post,* September 1, 1951, p. 19.

Chapter Ten

1. Josh McDowell, *Evidence That Demands a Verdict,* p. 193.
2. Ibid., p. 233

Chapter Eleven

1. *Time*, December 13, 1976, p. 93.
2. Ibid., E-3, p. 94.
3. Thomas Harris, *I'm OK—You're OK* (London: Cape. 1973)
4. Sergiu Grossu, *The Church in Today's Catacombs* (New Rochelle, N.Y.: Arlington House Publishers, 1975), p. 43.
5. Sheila Ostrander and Lynn Schroeder, *Psychic Discoveries Behind the Iron Curtain* (Englewood

Cliffs, N.J.: Prentice-Hall, 1970), pp. 151 ff.

6. John Hunter, *Impact* (Glendale, Calif.: Regal Books, 1966), pp. 45, 46.

7. Oswald Chambers, *My Utmost for His Highest* (London: Marshall, Morgan & Scott, 1972)

Chapter Twelve

1. Hannah Whitall Smith, *The Christian's Secret of a Happy Life* (London:

Lakeland Pubs.)

2. Francis A. Schaeffer, *He Is There and He Is Not Silent* (London: Hodder & Stoughton, 1972)

3. J. I. Packer, *Knowing God* (London: Hodder & Stoughton, 1975)

Chapter Thirteen

1. Hannah Whitall Smith, *The Christian's Secret of a Happy Life*